Facing Your Anxiety

A Personal Guide to Freedom from Anxiety

JACQUELINE Y. CHU

Facing Your Anxiety: A Personal Guide to Freedom from Anxiety.

Jacqueline Y. Chu

Note

The names and identifying details have been changed to protect the privacy of those mentioned in this book.

This book is not intended to replace or contradict the advice of health care professionals. It is designed to be an informative guide for those interested in learning more about and improving their mental health and wellbeing.

Why do you stay in prison when the door is so wide open?

— Rumi

Table of Contents

1

Anxiety Is Personal

Standing in the subway during rush hour, my friend casually commented that we were late for our meeting. Thoughts suddenly flooded my mind: *I can't believe I'm late again. What's wrong with me? Why can't I do anything right? I'm not good enough. I was never good enough.* Something felt terribly wrong. My heart started racing even though I was standing still. I felt frozen, and my body was refusing to move like it wasn't mine. At the same time, I felt so restless to the point it took everything to stop myself from running away to hide somewhere alone. From then on, my life was never the same.

I got through the meeting somehow, but as soon as I pulled myself out of there, I disappeared into a deserted building. I desperately needed to be alone, so I could think, and so no one would see me like this. I sat there for hours trying to calm down, but the intense thoughts and feelings only worsened. The harder I tried to think, the more trapped I felt in my head. There was no way out of this. *I must be going crazy,* I thought. *Nothing happened. I was just going to a meeting. There is no reason for me to be like this.* I couldn't make sense of what was happening. Anxiety came out of nowhere for me. I was a law student at the time.

It was years later that I realized that I had been having an anxiety attack and that it was a long time coming because I had lived with chronic anxiety since I was young and didn't even know it was anxiety. Anxiety to me was like water to fish. Oddly enough, my therapists never specifically focused on helping me with anxiety, even though I had worked with many over the years. The focus had always been on depression. Anxiety, which I believe was a significant underlying cause for depression, went undiagnosed and untreated.

Why was my anxiety able to fly under the radar? I believe it's because it took the form of various insecurities like perfectionism, self-doubt, and self-criticism. I didn't like myself much and was used to treating myself harshly and pushing myself to the edge to achieve and accomplish. I could care less about my health and wellbeing. I never had to use the term anxiety to describe my pains. Besides, for a long time, I didn't appear to have a problem because I was rewarded for my insecurities, which kept me on my toes, with excellent grades, impressive achievements for my resume, and admiration of those around me. Until anxiety manifested into physical symptoms, I thought I was doing just fine. Only later did I realize that I had struggled with anxiety all along, and my insecurities were intricately linked to anxiety. And it was only after I became a therapist that I realized just how many people were suffering the way I did and carrying on as if all was fine.

When I first heard the term anxiety, I didn't know that it had anything to do with me. Anxiety is estimated to affect about one in five of the population at a given time.[1] Yet, we all experience anxiety differently. We can label it as "social anxiety," but everyone has different reasons why they experience it. Here is a small sample of what I helped my clients uncover that led them to their struggle with social anxiety:

- "Growing up, my mom was ashamed to introduce me to her friends because of my body weight. She was happy to show off my sister, who was thin and pretty."
- "I grew up in a small town where I was the only visible minority. I felt different and undesirable."
- "I was diagnosed with a learning disability that makes me hard to read social cues."
- "I blush easily, and it's really embarrassing when it happens."
- "I'm sensitive and feel too stimulated in group settings."
- "My parents fought a lot, and it made me feel scared and anxious as a child on a daily basis."

When we try to address anxiety, we often make the mistake of treating it as "just anxiety." There are countless tools, techniques,

---

[1] "Any Anxiety Disorder," National Institute of Mental Health, accessed January 20, 2023, https://www.nimh.nih.gov/health/statistics/any-anxiety-disorder.

and even medications for treating anxiety. Many are widely available at our fingertips thanks to the internet: deep breathing, yoga, meditation, emotional freedom technique, and cognitive behavioral therapy (thought records), to name just a few. While these may help decrease the severity of anxiety symptoms, they cannot get to the root of what is as complex as *your* anxiety. Trying to treat anxiety without a deep understanding of your anxiety is like taking Tylenol to treat a cavity in your tooth. It helps but only temporarily at the surface level.

Despite what we may have been led to believe about mental health, we can't delegate treatment of your anxiety to a professional like how we can sit back as our dentists treat our cavities. If we do that, we make the same mistake of using tools to address surface-level symptoms. Whether or not we choose to work with a professional or do it alone, we need to face our anxiety head-on to understand what's beneath it. Then, the daily insecurities we experience, such as perfectionism, procrastination, and comparing (and despairing), will begin to make sense.

Knowing why we suffer from anxiety doesn't necessarily heal us from it. But it's an essential first step. If you are often haunted by the pain of anxiety and want to heal the pain, you need to become your own therapist, which means listening with empathy and without judgment, holding yourself in high regard with an attitude of acceptance, and encouraging yourself to learn and utilize therapeutic skills and tools.

When working with a new client, I don't start by teaching tools and techniques to cope with anxiety. I first listen so I can understand and appreciate them as a person and the specific issues they are dealing with. Likewise, you also need to ask yourself questions and listen with empathy before you start offering suggestions to yourself. It doesn't stop there. You must understand and accept who you are as a person and where you are in your journey. Then, only then, you are ready to hear the message that you have anxiety, it's not supposed to be dangerous, and these are some ways you can start feeling better.

Do you have an old emotional pain you've been trying to eliminate? Perhaps you've been bullied as a child or as an adult and have been attempting to move past it. You may have told yourself, "It happened long ago, and I should be over it now." Have you also blamed yourself for having anxiety and failing to have it under control? But it's not that easy and straightforward. Otherwise, you would've done it by now. Treating ourselves with impatience and making demands don't help.

In this book, I'll share how to get to know yourself and your anxiety to the point that it feels as familiar and harmless as a friend. Then, I'll show you easy-to-learn tools and techniques so you can free yourself from anxiety by breaking the patterns and retraining your mind. If your default state was anything like mine years ago (i.e., always anxious), you'll soon start noticing shifts and changes. You'll be able to tell when you are anxious because you'll know what it's like to feel calm and relaxed. When you do feel anxious, you'll be able to use your new skills to shift out of the anxious state. When you do this repeatedly, your default state will change over time until you no longer identify with the statement, "I'm an anxious person." It'll be more like, "I feel anxious sometimes, and it's okay. I've got this."

Our goal is to transcend anxiety by facing it head-on. In other words, it's about becoming greater than anxiety so that it becomes small and insignificant. A while ago, I worked with Vicky, who suffered from anxiety to the point that she believed she wasn't capable of anything, and her family walked on eggshells around her, treating her like a child. During the first few sessions, I focused on showing Vicky how she had come to form the belief she wasn't capable and how that belief wasn't true. I helped her see that having challenges and struggles doesn't mean that she was flawed as a person. She gradually began to see the smart, caring, and capable person she has always been. We discussed how it wasn't necessary to wait to start living until she was smarter and in better physical shape and that it was possible to start accepting herself for who she is, was, and will be all at the same time.

Vicky started to understand and advocate for herself, her insecurities diminishing. I showed her the tools and techniques I've used personally to free myself from anxiety. The more she used the new skills, the more she felt capable and back in control. Success begets success, and Vicky was building all the right momentum. Soon enough, she was doing all the things she had been scared of, like going out with friends, going on an overseas trip by herself, and making a career change. Vicky now treats anxiety for what it is, a passing feeling or state that she can work with, not something to be afraid of.

Another client, Fred, came to me after suffering from a severe anxiety attack that prevented him from returning to work. Although he wanted his anxiety gone right away, the first step was to face it, spending some time understanding and processing where his anxiety was coming from. Together we uncovered that he had trouble trusting his abilities (despite having the full confidence of his boss and colleagues at his firm) and dreaded letting people down; he wanted to keep his image of being perfect, like a robot.

He worked diligently with me to get to know himself better and set a firm intention for a life more aligned with his values. He began to appreciate himself for being a kind, caring, and genuine person and realized how much he enjoyed authentically connecting with people, which helped him let go of the idea of being a perfect robot.

Once the foundational work was done, working with anxiety became much easier. With the help of the tools and techniques I shared with him, Fred learned to see anxiety as something that he experienced from time to time, not an illness or who he was as a person. Being able to guide himself from an anxious, activated state to a stable, relaxed state regularly gave him confidence that he was freeing himself from anxiety and he could continue on his journey of becoming more and more true to himself.

You Can Stop Fixing Yourself: Freedom from Anxiety

I had spent most of my life running away from myself. It often was in the form of reading an endless array of self-improvement books. They were my friends, guides, and gurus. They provided a hope for a better future that I could finally fix myself and exist in peace. I remember when I was obsessed with reading about how to talk to anyone, make friends, and carry conversations with ease. What I didn't know was that I had social anxiety. I knew I felt uncomfortable in the presence of others, and I just wanted to make the feeling disappear by improving my social skills. During that time, never once did I think of the idea that I could face my anxiety head-on and actually get to know, accept, and like myself. Instead, I just kept on fixing myself: If I looked better, spoke better, and was more disciplined, articulate, smarter, athletic, efficient, etc., then I'd feel confident. But the promise of confidence and inner security never materialized through self-improvement. As I write these words, I feel compassion for my younger self and others who have felt the same way: flawed and broken, in need of fixing.

Do you find yourself haunted by anxiety to hide and fix your "flaws"? Do you struggle to be perfect so no one can criticize you and so you don't feel like you aren't good enough? Facing your anxiety, not fixing yourself, is the way out of this vicious cycle.

Anxiety is here to lead you out of a life of limits and constraints so you can fully be you. Your work with anxiety isn't about anxiety. It's about you learning to be greater than your emotions and challenges, in other words, transcending anxiety and freeing yourself once and for all.

Freedom from anxiety is a topic that's truly close to my heart. This book is personal. I remember the days I felt hopeless and helpless because I couldn't see a way out. When I was a lawyer, I remember feeling sick to my stomach and wanting to run away when I spoke on behalf of my clients in court. I thought I was doomed to suffer from anxiety for the rest of my life. This is the book I wish I had had during that time. Spending more than a decade helping myself and others free themselves from anxiety has taught me that there definitely is a way out, and it does not have to take years of therapy or some sort of innovative treatment.

Many of my clients achieve significant relief from anxiety in as little as one to twelve sessions because it's not about the time one spends in therapy. When people understand themselves and how their minds work, treat themselves with kindness and acceptance, and use skills that empower them, it becomes impossible for anxiety to run their lives. They become much greater than their anxiety. They can't help but put anxiety in its place, a passing feeling that's normal for anyone to experience from time to time.

In this book, you will discover a way out of a life run by anxiety. Here are some great results you'll achieve by following this framework and doing the work:

- increased self-awareness
- understanding your unique challenges and triggers
- increased self-acceptance and self-compassion
- identifying anxiety and stopping it on its track before it takes over
- unlearning the habits that drive anxiety
- shifting away from anxious by default to calm and relaxed
- using techniques to break the patterns of anxiety
- using self-hypnosis to empower yourself and create desired positive outcomes

Anxiety is not the enemy. Imagine that it's an annoying friend who showed up in your life to help guide you to a better life. That's how it played out for my clients and me. I've lost count of people who said at the end of our work that they are grateful for anxiety because it led them to a journey of self-discovery, acceptance, and growth that they wouldn't otherwise have pursued. Patience is key here. You may feel frustrated about your current affliction, but know that you'll get there sooner or later. Anxiety is most certainly not an incurable, lifelong diagnosis that some people and even some professionals may have led you to believe. This book will equip you with the knowledge and tools necessary to help you overcome your anxiety and change how you work with difficult emotions and circumstances in your life. But more importantly, once you allow yourself to keep an open mind, your journey with anxiety will help you develop a more loving relationship with yourself and pave the way to a joyful life and freedom to live your life unrestricted by anxiety.

2

Why You Still Feel Anxious

"I feel like I'm a failure."

"Well, let's look at what failure is, shall we?" my therapist asked me with curiosity and playfulness in his voice. He handed me a writing pad and a pen. After a short brainstorming session on the meaning of failure, I came up with this: Failure means giving up. I haven't given up and never will, so I'm not a failure.

It all made sense logically. My lawyer brain enjoyed every moment of the exercise and the conclusion. I knew I shouldn't feel like a failure. But why do I still feel like I'm a massive failure? Why do I continue to feel anxious every time I step into the courtroom? Even though I had found the right conclusion, my mind refused to believe I didn't need to feel anxious. It was frustrating.

When we encounter mental health challenges like anxiety and depression, we often try to think ourselves out of the quagmire. Many people have internal dialogues that resemble the following:

"I shouldn't feel _____ [insert emotion – e.g., anxious, sad, guilty]

because _____ [insert a reason]."

Here are some examples:

"I shouldn't feel depressed because I have so much to be grateful for, marriage, a well-paying job, friends, etc."

"I should be more confident because I got a good performance review and my boss always tells me I'm doing a good job."

"I can't stop thinking about my mistake, but it shouldn't matter because they probably forgot about it already."

Even though the statements are objectively true and reasonable, they don't necessarily help us feel better. Despite our good intentions, we end up feeling the same way or even worse because it doesn't make sense why we continue to feel crappy with all the evidence pointing towards the conclusion that we shouldn't.

Here are some reasons why knowing the right information or solution often doesn't help us overcome chronic anxiety.

1. Your unconscious mind doesn't buy it.
2. Learning takes practice.
3. Motivation and willpower aren't enough.
4. We habitually respond to the same stimuli (triggers) with the same thoughts, feelings, and behaviors.
5. There are physiological reasons for your anxiety.

1. Your unconscious mind doesn't buy it.

Whatever we think and feel comes from a bigger source: the unconscious mind, which lives outside your consciousness. The unconscious mind is like an iceberg. We can't see what's underneath our thoughts and feelings, but we know and sense it's there. The unconscious mind encompasses everything we've experienced in our lifetime, whether or not we consciously remember it. While it's easy to craft positive thoughts, they will be rejected in your mind if they are inconsistent with your beliefs in your unconscious mind. That's when you feel that what you think and feel don't match.

Consider this example. I consciously know that I fear failure and how it makes me feel anxious. I try to talk myself out of my anxiety by telling myself, "I'm not going to fail. I practiced a lot. Even if I fail, it's not a big deal." In the meantime, somewhere in my unconscious mind is a memory of being made fun of in third grade for giving a wrong answer to a teacher's question. It's not just a snapshot of a memory. The unconscious mind remembers vividly and in detail how my body went rigid when all the kids started laughing, the shame I felt, and how I told myself never to put myself out there like that. It is a powerful memory. My words of encouragement to myself are not enough to convince my unconscious mind to ignore or let go of this traumatic experience and feel at peace.

You might find it frustrating that changing your unconscious mind is difficult, but it's not necessarily a bad thing. If we could change our beliefs right away based on any information we encounter, that would cause some serious problems. We'd have no trouble believing one conspiracy theory after another. We'd have zero protection against scammers. Thankfully, the unconscious mind is like a "bouncer" that lives in our minds, deciding which information gets to enter and become a belief.

The problem is that we don't get to consciously decide which information to let into or keep out of our unconscious minds. Even though you may think that feeling more confident is good for you and you should start believing that you are confident, your unconscious mind may disagree because, for example, it thinks that you may do something reckless and make a fool of yourself by feeling confident.

To make lasting positive changes as we are doing here with your anxiety, we must find ways to bypass the "bouncer" and let new positive beliefs into our unconscious mind. Unless we do that, all attempts to think ourselves out of anxiety will fail.

2. Learning takes practice.

Learning something takes more than reading or hearing about it. Knowing something doesn't mean you've learned it. You may know all about how to play baseball, but it doesn't mean you know how to play if you've never thrown a ball before. You can read about how to build a computer, but that doesn't mean you can build one yet. Now that you know how you are *supposed to* do it, it's time to start practicing and *actually* do it. You'll have to go and buy some parts and start putting them together. You'll likely make mistakes along the way, and the computer won't turn on or work as it should. However, if you keep at it, you'll eventually be able to build a computer that works as it should. Next time you build a computer, you'll find it easier and be more knowledgeable about the parts and the process.

The same goes for learning how to overcome chronic anxiety. Once you've gathered the information, you have to start practicing and applying it in your life. Otherwise, you haven't really learned it, and the new knowledge will be mostly useless, like the random facts we know that don't improve our lives—did you know that fish can cough?

Practicing diligently can be challenging. Anxiety drains our energy and overwhelms us with fear, making it difficult to apply anything we learn. We can push our way through, but one tough day at work or one bad fight with our partners can throw us off track. It may make us want to give up trying because we feel exhausted.

3. Motivation and willpower aren't enough.

As discussed above, it takes conscious effort to learn new skills. When we feel constantly overwhelmed, terrified, depressed, etc., there isn't much capacity left in us to work towards making changes. Facing and transcending anxiety involves thinking, feeling, and doing things differently. It's like overhauling how your mind operates. Have you ever seen a notification that pops up just before upgrading your smartphone or laptop, indicating, "Make sure the device has at least 50 percent battery left or is plugged into a power source"? Upgrading your mind also takes time, energy, and inner resources, such as willpower. Motivation helps you get started but isn't a reliable resource because it comes and goes.

Let's talk about motivation. You may have started reading this book thinking *I'm done living like this. I'm going to overcome anxiety. I'll do this for myself (and perhaps others) and improve my life. I got this!* You have the momentum, and it feels like you can do it, no problem. You are motivated. It feels like a certainty that you'll absorb the knowledge presented here, do all the exercises, and apply everything you learn. But alas, if you've ever made a new year's resolution before, you know what it's like to fall off track. Motivation comes and goes.

Willpower can be defined as the state of being in charge of one's own behavior, feelings, and impulses. As much as we'd like to, we do not have unlimited willpower. It works more like a battery and has limits. When trying to break out of chronic anxiety, your mind will naturally want to engage in old habitual patterns, making you want to think, feel, and act the way you are used to. Your mind will naturally want to worry, catastrophize, procrastinate, and criticize yourself if those were your habits. One way to stop yourself is to use willpower and tell yourself, "Stop! This isn't good for me." However, when willpower is the only resource you can count on to keep yourself from falling back into these unhelpful old patterns, you'll quickly deplete your willpower and feel exhausted. You need something more than willpower and motivation to create sustainable changes for yourself.

4. We habitually respond to the same stimuli (triggers) with the same thoughts, feelings, and behaviors.

We are creatures of habit. We live our daily lives out of habit because our brains are naturally wired to think, feel, and act the same way about the events we encounter in our lives that we've experienced before. It's a mechanism of efficiency. When our brains work automatically like this, it saves us the time and energy it takes for us to go through the events as if it's our first time.

For someone who feels anxious about presentations, it may go like this:

Alex has a big presentation coming up in two weeks. She starts feeling anxious and decides to do something fun, like watching her favorite show to distract herself. As the deadline approaches, she starts to feel even more anxious and finds herself thinking about all the terrible what-if scenarios. "What if I make a mistake in front of everyone, and someone calls me out? What if someone asks me a question I don't know how to answer? What if I stutter or blush during the presentation? I don't want to look stupid. I'm not good enough."

Alex's anxiety peaks on the day of the presentation, and she feels like throwing up and running away. She pushes through (because she's afraid of being fired) but feels so self-conscious during the presentation that she has difficulty focusing on the materials. She finds herself thinking, "I never want to do this again. I'm no good at this." When it's over, her anxiety dissipates. While she feels a sense of relief, her body feels limp and exhausted from all the stress. She just wants to go home and lie down.

Public speaking is part of Alex's job, and she has to present regularly. This same set of thoughts, feelings, and actions is most likely to repeat itself next time she has to present. Even if Alex has read books and watched videos on overcoming presentation anxiety, as soon as she starts to feel anxious about the next presentation, she'll have a strong urge to create the same chain reaction.

To overcome her *habit* of anxiety, she'll need specific skills to recognize and break the cycle that keeps her trapped, reacting the same way over and over again to the stimulus of doing a presentation.

5. There are physiological reasons for your anxiety.

Last but not least, there may be physiological reasons for your anxiety. Our bodies and minds are not separate. If our bodies are anxious, our minds are anxious too. Jessie, a chronic anxiety sufferer, only realized how much calmer she felt after significantly cutting down on coffee and energy drink consumption. She then created some space to make even more changes to help herself out of anxiety. Medical conditions and side effects of medications can also affect our anxiety levels.

Here are some common physiological factors for anxiety:

- Caffeine consumption (coffee, tea, energy drinks, chocolate, etc.)
- Sleep problems
- Medical conditions (such as thyroid problems and diabetes)
- Medications
- Drugs/substance use (including alcohol)
- Hormones
- Diet and eating issues

While it doesn't mean that you'll continue to struggle with anxiety as long as you have these issues, it would be helpful to take inventory of your physical health and do what you can to make appropriate changes to help yourself. You can, for example, adopt a better bedtime routine by refraining from eating and looking at screens late at night to help improve sleep.

Begin to Change Through Awareness and Acceptance

It takes self-awareness to recognize and understand our patterns before they start running our lives for us. Without self-awareness, we are likely to fall into the above traps repeatedly. Then, it takes self-compassion to accept yourself regardless of your flaws and shortcomings. Acceptance is the beginning of change. In my experience as an anxiety-sufferer and professional healer, no good lasting changes were born out of self-hatred. Hating your shortcomings only breeds more anxiety.

My clients frequently tell me they don't know how to change. Often, we can see our patterns clearly, but there is no acceptance. We hate being stuck in a cycle and want to get out RIGHT NOW. But what if our cycle is here to teach us something about ourselves and show us a better life? What if it's not about the destination (i.e., an anxiety-free life) but the journey that will improve our lives? Our struggles can serve as portals to a better life if we allow them to. It all starts with acceptance.

Getting to acceptance isn't easy, but very doable. In chapters five and six, I'll show you the exact process to help you develop self-awareness and acceptance. The skills you develop through the process will serve as a strong foundation for the anti-anxiety techniques you'll learn later.

Jane came seeking help with anxiety and stress which had skyrocketed since starting to work as an investment banker at a top firm. She worked long hours and spent most of her time at her office. Due to the nature of her industry, working less and spending more time on self-care was unfortunately not feasible for Jane even though they would have made a big difference in her well-being. We needed to work with what we had.

At first, all we could do was damage control. Jane needed someone to talk to. She worked long days, all week, and weekends except for half a day on weekends, feeling immersed in anxiety, and she felt that our therapy sessions were the only opportunities she had to vent and be herself. Otherwise, Jane was in performance mode, trying to keep up with the image of being perfectly capable and bright. In the beginning, she walked away from sessions feeling a bit better, and with more tools under her belt, her overall level of anxiety had shifted only a little.

Thankfully, she didn't give up. Each time we met, we created a bit more space, and breathing room for her to get to know and accept herself. She reflected on what it was like to grow up overseas as a visible minority and how she had been carrying a sense of being different, an outsider, and shame, even though she knew intellectually that there was no need to feel shame.

In a courageous move, she resolved to accept her past and how it related to her anxiety in the present and to work towards unconditionally accepting herself for who she is (even though it had initially felt impossible). Since then, Jane began to increasingly identify anxiety as passing feelings that she experienced rather than an ever-present state. She worked to break the habit of anxiety by neutralizing her triggers one by one, skillfully using reflection, acceptance, and tools.

Have you tried to overcome anxiety with the help of therapy, self-help books, and various information you find on the internet, only to feel overwhelmed by obstacles and unable to apply what you've learned effectively? Life can throw curve balls, and our busy schedules can make it impossible to dedicate enough time and attention to treating a condition as complex as your anxiety. I say "complex" because while we can label the condition as "anxiety," which is common across the globe, we need to pay attention to treating *you* as a person instead of treating anxiety. This is why freedom from anxiety isn't typically achieved by taking meditations or changing up your routines.

I can assure you that you can free yourself from anxiety, and it doesn't need to take years of therapy to dig up and heal all your wounds from the past. What it takes is an open mind and curiosity to explore, understand, and begin to accept yourself and learn new (including perhaps some "strange" or unfamiliar) skills to work with anxiety effectively. You'll get to know yourself and your anxiety intimately, and soon you'll realize that, yes, it takes effort, sometimes a lot of effort, but it certainly is possible to live a life unconstrained by the burden of anxiety.

3

The Roadmap

At this point, you might ask, so how does this all work? How *exactly* and through what process will I overcome my anxiety? This chapter will give you a bird's eye view of the process, so you'll know what is ahead and how each part fits together in your journey to freedom from anxiety.

You may already have knowledge on some of these topics and have even tried the techniques in this book, such as mindfulness, to different degrees of success. I want to remind you not to lose sight of the forest for the trees. It's not the individual skills or techniques that will free you from anxiety but the shift in your overall relationship with yourself and your anxiety. You will benefit most when you take the time to get to know yourself first and what's behind your anxiety. Then, you can use different techniques as tools to effectively manage anxiety.

Think about the skills you've learned in the past and how you became good at them. How did you learn that? Likely not by trying to learn some advanced moves before you get the basics down. Let's take cooking, for example. There's a lot going on behind creating a delicious, beautifully presented dish. I was an ambitious beginner when I first tried to learn how to cook. I did my "research" by looking up some impressive recipes online and just dove in. The recipes I chose were very complicated with many ingredients and steps, which meant I ended up spending hours in the kitchen trying to figure out how to zest an orange and julienne carrots, whether to cut onions horizontally or vertically, and shifting through spices I've never smelled or tasted before. Totally overwhelmed, I somehow managed to create a dish that at least resembled the one in the picture. But it was exhausting and I had no fun at all cooking this way as I had no idea what I was doing. Then, I finally understood there was a better way. There was a whole theory behind creating flavors and a logical order to prepping the ingredients. I went back to the basics and learned why things are done in certain ways and the differences they make in how the food taste. This allowed me to stop relying on recipes as much because I had an understanding of how the dish I was about to cook was going to come together, rather than focusing on each step of the recipe and hoping the dish would be created as long as I faithfully followed each step. I now keep my sight on the forest, not the trees.

If cooking isn't your jam, consider how you'd learn to invest in the stock market. Would your first move be to read a few blog posts and jump into day trading? Knowing how to day trade can certainly be a helpful skill in your overall investment portfolio, but first, you'll want to learn how it fits in the bigger context of investing. You'll first want to know how the market works, different types of stocks, how to research the right companies to invest in, how to review financial statements and the psychology of investing, among other necessary background knowledge and techniques. Without at least some basic understanding of the overall picture, jumping into day trading relying on just a few techniques will likely prove risky and unprofitable.

Learning to overcome anxiety is like learning any other skill. Without a proper understanding of the complete picture, practicing breathing techniques in isolation can only do so much to help with your anxiety. It's just a step in the recipe to freedom from anxiety. Any techniques you'll learn in this book (or elsewhere, for that matter) need to be used contextually with the knowledge of their purpose. As you go through the book, remember how each part fits in the context you are working with: understanding and accepting yourself, learning how your mind and anxiety work, and effectively using the skills to retrain your mind.

My journey with anxiety was tumultuous, and it often felt like I was taking a few steps forward only to backtrack repeatedly. My motivation and willpower waned and provided little help for consistent progress. I tried many things. They were unfortunately out of context and in an order that didn't make sense because I was desperate and would do anything not to feel the way I did back then. I had success with certain things like mindfulness but wondered why I still struggled with anxiety despite my progress.

When I finally crossed the line from "managing anxiety" to "anxiety is no longer my issue," I began to see the big picture. Applying my learnings to clinical work, I developed a framework that can also help you cross the line. The materials and exercises in this book are designed to engage your unconscious mind so that you can develop new powerful beliefs that will help you overcome anxiety. I also promise you won't have to rely on motivation and willpower if you follow this framework.

The Road to Freedom from Anxiety

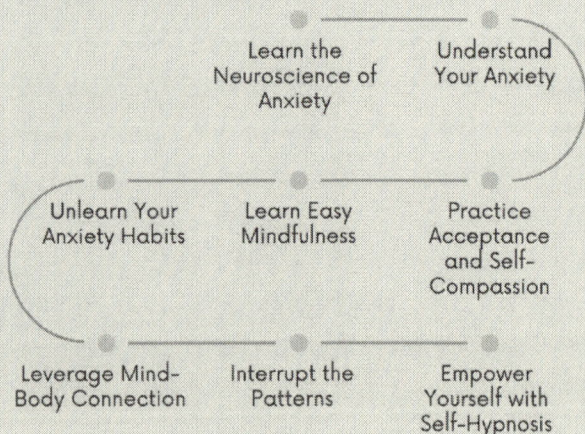

- Learn the Neuroscience of Anxiety
- Understand Your Anxiety
- Unlearn Your Anxiety Habits
- Learn Easy Mindfulness
- Practice Acceptance and Self-Compassion
- Leverage Mind-Body Connection
- Interrupt the Patterns
- Empower Yourself with Self-Hypnosis

Neuroscience of Anxiety

You may know intuitively what anxiety is and feels like. Even though everyone's anxiety is different, we all share the same neuroscience of how anxiety happens in our brains and nervous system.

Some background knowledge will help you as you continue on your journey. Lack of knowledge generates fear. Back in the day, people believed that the earth was flat, and sailors were afraid to go too far for fear they would fall off the earth and die. This fear quickly disappeared when the myth was disproved. People also commonly used to think that diseases were punishments from God and we had no power or control over how to prevent or heal ourselves. Once we could study diseases, defining them as bacteria and viruses, we could take measured steps to treat and prevent diseases. Starting your journey with the objective knowledge of anxiety will help you see it for what it is so you can start to let go of the fear of feeling anxious.

In Chapter 4, Neuroscience of Anxiety, we'll explore what anxiety is, what happens in our bodies when we are anxious, and some everyday examples of what anxiety looks like when broken down process by process.

Facing Your Anxiety

While how anxiety happens in our bodies looks similar from person to person, the specific content of anxiety is always different—the content of your specific thoughts, feelings, physical sensations, and beliefs associated with anxiety. By observing them closely, you'll notice some repeating patterns and what lies under the patterns.

Getting to know your anxiety intimately like this will help clear up any fears of anxiety even further. We fear what we don't know or don't have control over. When you actively study your anxiety rather than avoid it, you are letting your mind know you are in control and anxiety is not to be feared. You'll want to get your journal or a pen and paper handy, as there will be self-reflection exercises you can follow along with.

In Chapter 5, Facing Your Anxiety, we look at your triggers and what's driving *your* anxiety.

Acceptance and Self-Compassion

Key skills of acceptance and self-compassion are essential for you to learn in order to overcome anxiety. Would it surprise you that most of your anxiety is caused and exacerbated by an inability to accept and lack of empathy for yourself? In my personal and clinical work, I've observed developing the skills of acceptance and self-compassion to be what usually makes the biggest difference.

All positive changes begin with acceptance, and acceptance requires self-compassion. Often, my clients tell me they don't know how to be kind to themselves. Sometimes, they are hesitant even to begin because they don't want to "coddle and spoil" themselves. Thankfully, self-compassion has nothing to do with coddling, and in Chapter 6, I'll show you why and how it works.

Easy Mindfulness

Mindfulness is a foundational skill that makes all the other skills you'll learn in this book even more effective. For our purposes, we'll define mindfulness as bringing yourself back to the present and noticing your thoughts, feelings, and sensations as an observer. When mindful, you are less prone to being sucked into the whirlwind of your inner anxious thoughts. Developing mindfulness allows you to stay centered and intentionally choose your thoughts and actions despite how you might be feeling. It also enhances your ability to focus and practice what you learn.

While the benefits of mindfulness are well-known and well-researched, the problem is that we often find it hard to meditate, which is the primary method for cultivating mindfulness. Many people try to meditate regularly using free or paid apps and guided meditation recordings but unfortunately fall off track after a while. It's very much like exercising; we all know it's good for us, but doing it daily is another thing. Life gets in the way.

Chapter 7, Easy Mindfulness, addresses this issue. I'll show you what mindfulness is and isn't and how to develop and strengthen mindfulness in your daily life, even if you cannot meditate for a long time. I'll also show you some fun, easy ways to meditate so that you can look forward to rather than dread your meditation sessions.

Unlearning Your Anxiety Habits

Chronic anxiety is a habit of the mind. What do you do when you first wake up? Do you have a specific way you brush your teeth? How do you walk, left foot or right foot first? Chances are you do these things without even being aware that you are doing them in a certain way. If you've struggled with anxiety for a while, you likely engage in certain habits that kickstart, fuel, and intensify your anxiety. The four horsemen of anxiety are avoiding, worrying, what if-ing, and catastrophizing.

In Chapter 8, Unlearning Your Anxiety Habits, we'll consciously identify these harmful habits in your daily life that often go unnoticed unless we are on guard. You'll learn why they are harmful, how to stop them, and what to do instead. Unlearning these habits prevents us from making our anxiety worse, which you may realize is what you've been doing every day. Again, feeling anxious from time to time is not our issue. It is a normal part of life, and mild anxiety can even help us focus. It is the out-of-control anxiety that tries to run our lives, and just by eliminating the four horsemen of anxiety, you'll start to feel more in control of yourself.

Leveraging Mind-Body Connection

Our minds and bodies are inseparable. When our bodies relax, our minds relax, too, and vice versa. It's impossible to feel relaxed and anxious at the same time. When I was suffering from chronic anxiety, I rarely, if ever, felt relaxed. Only when I started playing soccer did I begin to notice what my body felt like when I was having fun and feeling relaxed. It was like a heavy burden had been lifted from my shoulders, and I wanted more of that, which resulted in me playing soccer seven days a week. Of course, a state of anxiety quickly returned after each game of soccer, and it took me some time to realize that I could actually create relaxation in my body at will with the help of the techniques I'll show you.

The point of the techniques is not just to feel relief from anxiety occasionally. Anxiety is like an addiction. Chronic anxiety floods us with stress hormones associated with fight or flight. These hormones are not meant to always be there because they wear us down, which is why stress leads to illnesses and chronic pain. Regularly using these techniques to relax will detox and destress your body so you can begin functioning better in your daily life.

In Chapter 9, Leveraging Mind-Body Connection, you'll learn techniques to help your body relax to turn the momentum from being primed for anxiety to being ready to face the day with more confidence and joy.

Interrupting the Patterns

Suffering from chronic anxiety means your brain is wired to be anxious. Your mind will *want* to feel anxious, and all brain pathways will lead there. In this state, feeling anxious is as easy as flipping a light switch because there is a wiring that connects a source of electricity (trigger) to the lightbulb (anxiety). Thankfully, this doesn't have to be permanent. We can change our brains by interrupting the patterns often and choosing to think, feel, and act differently. This concept is called neuroplasticity.

It's like a chain reaction. If you have health anxiety, for example, as soon as there is a trigger, such as a migraine, your mind will generate worrying thoughts, and you may start searching the internet, calling your doctor, and feeling restless. The actions are not helpful, but you feel you can't help it. It all feels automatic and out of control because you don't know when you'll be triggered, and once triggered, it always leads to the same result (anxiety and misery).

In Chapter 10, Interrupting the Patterns, you'll learn two techniques to easily and quickly interrupt your patterns and stop anxiety in its track. You'll experience two positive results over time when you frequently use the pattern interrupt techniques. First, you'll reclaim the power to influence your feelings, thoughts, and behaviors, thereby feeling more in control. Second, you'll gradually change the structure of your brain so you'll become more resilient to anxiety and stress and less likely to be triggered in the first place.

Empowering Through Self-Hypnosis

Self-hypnosis is my favorite technique, and I've used it to help myself in many areas: feeling more grounded and confident, improving my day-to-day mood, being a better communicator, being more patient in relationships, and improving sports performance, among many others. When you've worked through all the previous chapters, you'll have realized some ways you make yourself anxious. Anxiety is a state of self-hypnosis. If you can condition (hypnotize) yourself to feel anxious, you can also hypnotize yourself to be calmer and in control across different settings.

The opposite of anxiety is NOT "not anxious." If you had a choice, would you rather be "not anxious" or at peace, content, or even joyful? Your journey doesn't have to stop at being less anxious or not anxious. Your mind has the power to create positive states all on its own, and you can utilize the positive state to accomplish whatever you want, including but not limited to better relationships, making personal changes, and performing at your best.

In Chapter 11, Empowering Through Self-Hypnosis, I'll show you easy-to-use self-hypnosis techniques you can use to not only overcome anxiety but also make other positive changes in your life.

Summary

Here's a brief summary of the process. You'll first learn the objective and subject aspects of your anxiety. Then, you'll learn and practice the foundational skills of acceptance, self-compassion, and mindfulness and unlearn the habits that fuel anxiety. Lastly, you'll discover and practice various techniques to regain control and rewire your brain for resilience and calm.

Although it may seem like we have much to cover, I've designed the book to give you only the necessary information. I took the liberty of skipping unnecessary details so you can quickly start applying what you learn from day one. If you want to learn more about specific topics, I've included some suggested readings in the Appendix. This book will be short and to the point. To get the most out of this book, I recommend reading and applying the skills in the order they are presented rather than jumping around from chapter to chapter, as each chapter is intended to build on the previous chapters.

4

Neuroscience of Anxiety

There were about 20 of us gathered in our friends' one-bedroom loft. We were eating, drinking, and chatting in small groups when I started to notice I was feeling unwell. I sat down because I felt like my arms and legs were shaky. I had trouble focusing on what my friends were saying. My heart was racing, and so were the thoughts in my head. I felt my whole body becoming more and more tense. I had to get out of there. Fast.

I excused myself to speak to the host, a long-time friend who knew my struggles with mental health. I told her I wasn't feeling well, and she graciously offered their bedroom for me to rest alone without asking further questions. I went into the bedroom, shut the door, and sat on the floor, hugging my legs tightly.

"It's okay. It's just anxiety. It will pass."

Half an hour had passed when I came out of the bedroom, feeling traces of anxiety but much better.

Doesn't anxiety come at the most inconvenient time? It visits us when we are trying to do something important, make a good impression on someone, or just have a good time with friends, in my case. Sometimes, anxiety makes us avoid the activities that trigger it, which can really limit our ability to live and enjoy our lives.

When I had my first anxiety attack in law school, I stopped going to classes for a few weeks because when I sat in class, I felt like everyone was looking at and judging me. It sounds ridiculous, but it certainly felt true at the time. The anxiety I felt was unbearable. As I avoided more and more situations that made me anxious, my life became smaller and smaller, each day losing confidence in myself.

Things changed when I learned what anxiety was and that I had it. That night I went to the gathering, I knew that I might feel anxious. But I went anyway because I wanted to see my friends and, more importantly, because I had come to know that anxiety could be like any other illness. When I have a headache, I stop what I'm doing, pay attention to how my body is feeling, and take it easy by sitting or lying down. Unless it's particularly bad, I know it will pass, and I don't need to panic about it. I can also easily tell people I'm not feeling well and need to rest. Why should anxiety be any different?

I'd like you to think about your current relationship with anxiety. Are you often afraid of feeling anxious? Perhaps it's to the point that it stresses you out daily or causes you to miss out on life, from small to big things like parties, trips, friendships, dating, job opportunities, and even weddings. What would change if you were no longer afraid of anxiety? What would be the first thing you would do?

To help you take that first step towards freedom from anxiety, I'd like to share with you what anxiety is and how it works. If you feel anything like I did years ago, you may see anxiety as a terrifying beast that comes out of nowhere and that you have no control over once it shows up. Let's spend some time studying anxiety and clearing up any misconceptions. You'll see that anxiety is not the monster you thought it to be and perhaps more like a garden variety emotion that comes and goes.

These are the facts you need to know about anxiety so you can let go of the fear:

1. Anxiety is our body's response to a perceived threat.
2. While it can be very uncomfortable, anxiety is not dangerous.
3. Feeling anxious makes it more likely for us to feel anxious again.
4. We can change our brains to free ourselves from anxiety.

Anxiety and the Human Body

Anxiety results from how our bodies respond to perceived threats in our environment. It is a natural state necessary to help us escape danger and survive. Let's take a moment to understand what exactly happens in our bodies when we feel anxious.

First, let's define anxiety. Fear and anxiety are closely related. When we feel fear, it's generally acute and temporary. I used to be terrified of spiders (I still am a little afraid, if I'm being honest). When I went camping with a friend, I saw a big hairy spider inside our tent in the middle of the night. As soon as I saw it, I screamed, opened the tent, and ran out before I could even think. It didn't occur to me that other people in the campsite were sleeping or that my friend was still inside with the scary spider! Acute fear triggered my fight-or-flight response, and I fled. A few minutes later, when the spider was safely let out of the tent, I returned to reading as if nothing had happened.

In contrast to fear, we feel anxiety when the threat we perceive is NOT as well-defined or immediate as a spider in your tent. Job interviews, financial future, and marital issues are some examples. Unlike the threat of a spider, which can be neutralized by running away or taking it out (sorry, spider), these issues are more unpredictable, nebulous, and can't be easily removed. Anxiety is "a more long-lasting state of apprehension (sustained fear)."[2]

---

[2] Michael Davis et al., "Phasic vs Sustained Fear in Rats and Humans: Role of the Extended Amygdala in Fear vs Anxiety." *Neuropsychopharmacology* 35 (1): 105–35 (2010). https://doi.org/10.1038/npp.2009.109.

Let's break down what happens in our bodies, both in cases of acute fear and anxiety. There is an almond-shaped structure in your brain called the amygdala responsible for fear responses. Amygdala is an unconscious processor.[3] When my eyes perceived a spider, that sensory information was passed to the amygdala even before it reached the cortex (the thinking part of the brain).[4] The amygdala then triggered a rapid fight-or-flight response designed for survival, which resulted in my screaming and running away without thinking.

In the case of anxiety, the amygdala is also involved, but it doesn't make us react immediately. Our brains don't distinguish well between actual and imagined events. Say you are afraid of public speaking and have a presentation coming up. Even though the presentation is scheduled weeks away, by thinking about it, it becomes as if it's happening right now (at least from your brain's perspective). In response to this perceived threat, the amygdala sends signals to activate the sympathetic nervous system responsible for fight-or-flight and release stress hormones (cortisol and adrenalin) to mobilize your body. The heart rate as well as the blood sugar level go up. Even though the threat, in reality, is in the future, your body is already in fight-or-flight, ready for quick action.

---

[3] Joseph LeDoux, "The Amygdala." *Current Biology* 17 (20): R868–74 (October 2007). https://doi.org/10.1016/j.cub.2007.08.005.

[4] Catherine M. Pittman and Elizabeth M. Karle, *Rewire Your Anxious Brain: How to Use the Neuroscience of Fear to End Anxiety, Panic, & Worry* (Oakland: New Harbinger Publications, 2015), 21-22.

Anxiety also makes it hard for us to think clearly. When activated, the amygdala communicates with other regions of the brain, releasing various neurotransmitters[5] that affect the way we think. This can make us think even more anxiety-inducing thoughts, partly explaining why it's hard to think our way out of anxiety.

Anxiety is Not Dangerous

While anxiety is uncomfortable and causes wear and tear on our bodies over time, it is not dangerous. As you read earlier, we humans have a built-in system for dealing with threats (stress) in our environment. Have you ever had a fire alarm go off while sleeping or working? It's loud and disruptive, and it's meant to be that way so we drop everything and pay attention. Nevertheless, we've never met anyone who was hurt by a fire alarm. Hurt by a fire, maybe, but not by the alarm.

Anxiety is like a fire alarm. It is meant to signal that something is off and requires our attention for our safety. The problem is, just like faulty fire alarms that go off in the absence of fire or carbon monoxide, our anxiety signaling system can also become faulty and go off when it doesn't need to. When we keep this in mind, instead of panicking or reacting when our anxiety alarm goes off, we can carefully inspect whether it's a real "fire" or a false alarm.

---

[5] Sergio Linsambarth et al., "The Amygdala and Anxiety," in *The Amygdala - Where Emotions Shape Perception, Learning and Memories*, ed. Barbara Ferry (IntechOpen, 2017). https://app.dimensions.ai/details/publication/pub.1090370587.

In my story earlier, when I noticed my anxiety at the party, I was able to keep a cool head, knowing that it was just a signal, not necessarily a real danger. I created some time and space for myself to inspect and think, and I concluded that the anxiety might be due to the medication I had started to take. My friends weren't out to get me. There was no reason why I couldn't stay and still enjoy the night.

How We Learn and Unlearn the Anxiety Pathways in the Brain

We can leverage this knowledge to our advantage when we understand how our brains learn and unlearn anxiety. Our brains are always learning and changing from the moment we are born and as we go through life. This concept is called neuroplasticity: the brain's ability to change itself. The brain is composed of billions of cells called neurons that process information. The brain learns (i.e., we learn) when neurons form connections with one another.

Imagine you are trying to learn how to play tennis for the first time. You start by learning how to hold a racket. You hold it in a certain way, feel the racket in your hand, and note how it's positioned by looking at it. You give it a swing and adjust your grip as the racket shifts with each swing. All this time, your neurons are making new connections that didn't exist before.

How do they form connections with one another? This was explained by the phrase "neurons that fire together wire together," based on the work of psychologist Donald Hebb.[6] An easy way to understand this is to consider the famous experiment by Ivan Pavlov. By ringing a bell just before feeding a dog and repeating this over and over again, the researchers conditioned the dog to salivate whenever it heard the bell, even without food. The important thing to note is that in the dog's brain, there was initially no connection between the bell ringing and receiving food. The dog learned to associate the sound of the bell with food as they were paired together, neurons firing at the same time.

Likewise, the brain *learns* to associate anxiety with certain activities by repetitive conditioning. Let's look at an example. Mike has severe social anxiety. He is terrified of being in groups of people. He stays home and rarely goes out. But he remembers that it wasn't always like that for him. In middle school, he was athletic, outgoing, and popular. He enjoyed hanging out with friends and having a girlfriend.

Soon after he turned 15, his family decided to immigrate to Canada. Unfortunately, the kids and the teachers at his new school in the new country were far from friendly. They made fun of him for his looks and his accent. Mike began to feel more and more self-conscious of the way he dressed and spoke. Like every other student, he was required to go to school five days a week. Whenever he was at school, he felt anxious and worried that someone might harass him. Eventually, even the thought of

[6] Donald O. Hebb, *The Organization of Behavior: A Neuropsychological Theory* (New York: Wiley, 1949).

attending school and being around other kids filled him with dread and anxiety. Every time he experienced anxiety in response to school, the connection between school and anxiety in his brain got stronger. Neurons that fire together wire together.

The good news for Mike is that just as he learned social anxiety, he can also unlearn it. When neurons don't fire together, their connections become weaker. Have you ever tried to learn another language or take a language course at school? Most people forget much of what they learned soon after they stop actively studying the language. This is because you rarely use it unless you live in a country where that language is spoken. The neurons stop firing, and the connections wane. Therefore, Mike can also unlearn his social anxiety when he starts breaking his anxiety patterns associated with being around other kids. How he does this will be the subject of the rest of this book.

It had taken me some time to say, "It's just anxiety," because in the moment, anxiety can feel debilitating. But it was a game-changer when I understood what anxiety is and how it works in my body. For one, I no longer felt like something was seriously wrong with me. It was relieving to know that anxiety is our bodies' survival mechanism, an alarm system that we all have. My alarm system just happened to be more sensitive than the average. Learning about anxiety allowed me to start *observing* my anxiety as a separate concept instead of being sucked into it. This prepared me to learn different skills so that, eventually, I didn't need to temporarily shut down or go into hiding when I had anxiety.

Do you also sometimes beat yourself up for feeling anxious? What would it be like for you to say, "It's just anxiety"? One of my favorite moments in therapy is when my clients say, "I'm starting to feel more comfortable about being uncomfortable!" This tells me that they are letting go of their fear of anxiety, which means they are on the right track. By being "comfortable with being uncomfortable," they weaken the neural connections between anxiety and panic. Soon, they would also be able to say, "It's just anxiety," and carry on with their lives.

Nevertheless, we don't stop here. Getting to know anxiety is only the first step in your journey to freedom from anxiety. In the next chapter, you'll learn about *your* anxiety, more about yourself, and some ways you may have learned (and perhaps are still learning) to be anxious.

5

Facing Your Anxiety

I'm sitting in a church pew, feeling it all over my body. I don't know how it started, but it's here now. My shoulders are tight, and my chest is throbbing. I feel uneasy and like I need to go hide somewhere. I look to my left, and my boyfriend sits next to me, his eyes glued to the pastor. To my right, my best friend is reading her bible. I look around and see many friends scattered in the hall, people I just had lunch with and spoke to on the phone a few days ago.

Yet, I feel utterly alone. My thoughts are screaming, *I'm trapped. I need to get out of here right now.* I'm in a church pew, two rows from the front. There's no way I can get out without drawing attention. So I sit there helplessly and mentally checked out, my thoughts drifting to worst-case scenarios. I tell myself I should've never come here.

This was my anxiety. Whenever I went to a social gathering, there was a risk of being triggered. If I'm triggered, I'd feel trapped and feel crippling anxiety. It was a pattern that had repeated for over a decade since I was 13.

Given the number of times I had felt this way and repeated the same pattern, imagine how well-wired the neural pathways in my brain must have been. To change this longstanding pattern and find healing, I needed to understand where it came from and why.

Have you already noticed that your anxiety has patterns? It's often not too difficult to notice when something is wrong with us. You might think, "Yes, I know I have problems and where they come from. But how do I change and make them go away?"

Hold your horses! You may know your problems, but have you really taken time to listen to yourself with compassion and understand where your anxiety is coming from? To dismantle our unhealthy patterns and overcome anxiety, it is crucial that we first develop empathy for ourselves. Empathy comes from understanding. To understand, we need to listen.

Think about it this way. Say you had a really tough day at work. Your boss yelled at you for the mistakes you made in your report. You are feeling exhausted and not so good about yourself. You call a close friend to vent, and your friend says it's your fault for not paying enough attention to detail. She says you should work harder and double-check your work next time. How would you feel?

Now, what if, instead, it goes like this? She listens. She validates how you had a difficult day and reminds you that you've been working diligently to do a good job and support your team. Then, she asks you more questions about the report. She assures you that the mistakes weren't too big of a deal and gives you her perspective on how the mistakes may have been prevented. How would you feel after this interaction? If it were me, I'd feel much better and more motivated. Her words would matter to me because I know she knows, values, and understands me.

In the following two chapters, I'll show you how you can have encouraging, helpful interactions like this with yourself. The focus of this chapter is on *listening to* and *understanding* yourself. The next chapter will show you how to act on the understanding and translate it to compassion for yourself.

Please take out your journal[7] to record your responses to the following seven questions designed to help you get to know and understand *your* anxiety. If you are tempted to skip this, I strongly encourage you to do this exercise before you move on to the next chapters. This book is about helping you overcome *your* anxiety, so understanding your specific struggles is an essential piece of the puzzle that will help make sense of your anxiety.

---

[7] If you prefer to type, you can download the fillable PDF worksheets by accessing the resources at facingyouranxiety.com.

Writing down your answers is important because we'll need to review them at the end. Try to write as if you are describing your experience to someone else so they can understand.

Before we dive in, I'd like to offer you some words of caution and suggestions. Remember how I said in the previous chapter that our brains have a hard time telling the difference between an event that actually happened and an event we imagined happening? This applies to thinking about the past as well. When we remember a painful past event, it can lead to re-experiencing the pain and reinforcing the unhelpful anxious pathways in our brains.

To prevent this, we must put a different hat on. For this exercise, be a scientist. The subject you are examining is your anxiety. As a scientist, you must keep a certain distance from your subject. When you recall past events, try to keep a mental distance so you can be an observer. You can't observe clearly if you are busily re-experiencing the events. If you notice any discomfort during the exercise, you can stop, take a deep breath, and remind yourself of your intention to understand and overcome your anxiety.

7 Questions to Get to Know You and Your Anxiety

#1. When did you first start struggling with anxiety? What (if anything) happened?

We all have different reasons why we struggle with anxiety. You don't need to know exactly what triggered anxiety in the first place. Rather, this question allows us to reflect and start seeing patterns. Below are some answers given by my clients.

- "I've been anxious since starting to date my boyfriend. I keep thinking that bad things might happen to him and how I'd be all alone."
- "I started to feel really anxious after my divorce. I worry a lot about my kids and whether my ex will make up reasons to take them away from me."
- "I've never 'not had anxiety,' but anxiety got out of control after receiving a bad performance review. Since then, I've become so self-conscious at work that I can't stop thinking about how I might look to my boss and peers."
- "Starting my Ph.D. program has made me feel like an imposter and not smart enough to be here. I put a lot of pressure on myself to prove that I belong in the program."
- "Since turning 40, I've had death anxiety. I have a hard time focusing at work, and anxiety has spread to other areas of my life."

As you can see, the answers portray a variety of difficult circumstances. However, when my clients were given a chance to reflect further, they also remembered that anxiety didn't just come out of nowhere. Often, they had struggled for a long time without realizing it.

- "My parents told me I was a sensitive kid growing up. I was shy and afraid of everything."
- "I was always an anxious kid. As soon as I started school, I wanted to get the best grades. I don't think it mattered that much to my parents, but I always tried really hard to be the top student."
- "I remember hiding in my room a lot when my dad was drunk and my parents were arguing. This went on for years, at least a few times a week."

Now it's your turn. Recall when your struggle with anxiety intensified (likely a recent event) and when it may have started (when you were younger). Take some time to write down what comes to mind.

#2. When was the last time you felt anxious? What was going on externally and internally?

This time, pick a recent example to get a snapshot of what anxiety is like for you. Here's an answer from a client:

- "I was at a meeting with about eight people. We were discussing the upcoming project. My manager suddenly asked me to explain something to the group, and I froze. I stuttered and didn't know if my words made sense. I felt like I was put under a spotlight. I felt embarrassed and afraid I was going to say something wrong. I felt frozen."

You don't have to analyze and break down what happened. For now, describe the incident and what you were generally thinking and feeling as the incident unfolded. This is a warm-up exercise for the next question. You are practicing how to observe your anxiety.

#3. Think of another time you felt anxious. What were your symptoms? Categorize the symptoms into the following: physical sensations, feelings, thoughts, and behaviors.

We are getting into more detail now and honing your skills for observing your own internal processes. For this exercise, choose a time you had felt moderately anxious.

Here is an example:

- "I was attending a lecture and taking notes on my laptop when I started to feel anxious."

  Symptoms

  1. Physical sensations:
     - heart palpitations, sweaty palms, tight neck, jittery

  2. Feelings:
     - anxious, scared, ashamed

  3. Thoughts:
     - "I don't understand what the professor is saying. I feel stupid. What if the notes I take are pure

nonsense? People can see my screen. They are going to think I'm stupid. What if my friend asks me to borrow my notes? I want to get out of here."

4. Behaviors:
    • Didn't take notes
    • Packed up my stuff and left early
    • Didn't go to the next class

You can record sensations, feelings, thoughts, and behaviors in whichever order is easier for you to recall. If you start to feel anxious answering this question, remember that you are NOT re-experiencing it. You are in the here and now (wherever you might be) with this book and simply observing what happened in the past.

#4. What type of anxiety do you tend to struggle with? (e.g., social, performance, general, phobias)

Does your anxiety have a theme? While some people may struggle with anxiety about many different things, some experience anxiety in limited areas. For example, my client, who suffered from severe health-related anxiety, had no issues regarding social situations. Another client who is an engineer was only anxious in relationships ("people are unpredictable") and he rarely felt anxious when doing his job.

Here are some themes of anxiety and common symptoms. This is not a comprehensive list, so keep looking for themes and patterns of your anxiety if nothing listed here rings a bell.

Social anxiety

- Being self-conscious and anxious in social situations or relationships
- Worrying too much about how others might perceive you
- Going over your "mistakes" after the interaction is over

Performance anxiety

- Feeling anxious when you have to "deliver" results (e.g., presentations, assignments, public speaking, sports)
- Procrastinating, deferring, or trying to get out of having to do it

Generalized anxiety

- Feeling anxious in daily situations, even without specific triggers
- Chronic anxiety that feels constant
- Worrying about "little things"
- Difficulty relaxing even when nothing is happening

Phobias

- Anxiety is triggered by specific stimuli (e.g., elevators, spiders, heights)

#5. *What specific situations, settings, or people trigger anxiety?*

We are narrowing down your anxiety and looking at how it plays out in your daily life. Once you've got a sense of the big picture from the previous question, examine the details of the picture. We are looking for patterns. What specific situations, settings, or people make you feel anxious?

If it's hard to answer this question on the spot, think about some of the times you felt anxious and recall where you were, who you were with, and what happened. Here are some examples. Although some of the examples contain the reasons why anxiety is triggered, you don't need to know why at this point. Simply recall and write down any patterns in your anxiety you notice.

- "I feel anxious every time I go to a family gathering. I don't think I do enough for them, so I always feel like I'm letting them down."
- "Being in the office makes me anxious. I'm afraid of small talk. I don't know what to say."
- "When I hang out with this specific group of friends, I feel anxious. They are all successful, and I don't feel like I belong. I don't want to talk to them about what I've been up to."
- "Being around big personalities makes me anxious. I end up staying silent and looking like a loser."
- "When I'm one-on-one with someone, I don't know what to do, and I just feel anxious."

- "Being in a group setting is anxiety-provoking. I get self-conscious and uncomfortable."

This part is all subjective. As you may have noticed in the last two examples, while one person feels anxious being one-on-one with people but at ease in groups, another person feels comfortable one-on-one but anxious when in a group. We all experience anxiety in different ways.

When answering this question, make sure to put aside any judgments that may arise. There is nothing wrong with you. We all have reasons why certain situations, settings, and people make us feel anxious and uncomfortable. And you will learn to dismantle these patterns. For now, be an observer and focus on making an honest, accurate observation. Don't try to change anything; you'll do that work later.

#6. Think of some significant events in your life that may have contributed to your anxiety patterns.

What's your gut feeling about where your anxiety is coming from? Many people suffering from anxiety report that their caregivers also suffered from anxiety, and they witnessed it growing up. This brings up an interesting question of nature vs. nurture. While studies have found anxiety disorders to be moderately heritable,[8] [9] the full story is more intricate as the development of anxiety involves a complex interplay between your genes, your environment, adversities you've faced (e.g., childhood trauma), and psychological factors.[10]

To overcome anxiety, you don't need to know exactly where your anxiety comes from and how it forms in your mind. However, to develop empathy and compassion for yourself (the work we'll be doing in the next chapter), getting the context for your anxiety is helpful.

Look at the following examples and think about what events may have contributed to how you struggle with anxiety at this point in your life.

- "Growing up, I was always compared to my older brother. He was known in the family to be smart, capable, and headed to the big leagues. As for me, they said, 'He's a bit slow, so we'll see about this one.' Now I feel like I have to constantly try hard to prove myself."

---

[8] Michael G. Gottschalk and Katharina Domschke, "Genetics of Generalized Anxiety Disorder and Related Traits." *Generalized Anxiety Disorders* 19 (2): 159–68 (2017). https://doi.org/10.31887/dcns.2017.19.2/kdomschke.

[9] Andrew A. Bartlett, Rumani Singh, and Richard G. Hunter, "Anxiety and Epigenetics." *Advances in Experimental Medicine and Biology* 978: 145–66 (2017). https://doi.org/10.1007/978-3-319-53889-1_8.

[10] M. A. Schiele, and K. Domschke, "Epigenetics at the Crossroads between Genes, Environment and Resilience in Anxiety Disorders." *Genes, Brain and Behavior* 17 (3): e12423 (2017). https://doi.org/10.1111/gbb.12423.

- "I was bullied in school when I immigrated to Canada. The kids and even some of the teachers were racist. The only way I could feel safe was to be better than all of them. I made sure to let them know that I'm smart by getting good grades. When I played sports, I tried to dominate. It was easier back then to compete and be at the top. Now that I'm in a post-graduate program, I can't get to the top, no matter how hard I try. I don't feel safe just being average."

- "My mom was depressed when I was seven. She didn't eat or come out of her room for days. I didn't know what to do. I couldn't make her feel better. As an adult, I'm constantly watching over other people's feelings. When my partner doesn't look like he's having a good day, I get anxious and miserable."

Think of some events in your life that you think are connected to your anxiety in the present. Again, put on your scientist hat and observe from a detached stance. If an unbiased observer was looking at your life, which events would they pick out to be contributing factors to your anxiety?

#7. Reflecting on your answers, what patterns do you see in your anxiety?

Now it's time to bring it all together. Spend some time reading your answers to each question, and you'll start noticing some patterns of your anxiety. It's possible you've already started to see and write down the patterns as you answered the previous six questions. For good measure, review all your answers and see what other insights jump out at you.

As much as you can, continue to observe from a scientist's perspective. This is the big secret to why therapists can do their jobs. They are outsiders to your problems, and thus it's easier for them to see other people's patterns. When it comes to our own problems, our judgment is often clouded by unhelpful thoughts and emotions (e.g., What's wrong with me? How do I fix this? I hate feeling this way). Stay in the present for now. Set aside all other thoughts and focus on looking for patterns. We are going one step at a time.

The patterns you observe can be as few or many as you notice. There are no right or wrong answers here. What insights have you gained? What do you now understand about *your* anxiety?

Take as much time as you need to complete this exercise. Write your reflections and insights in your journal. We'll take them with us to the next chapter. You don't have to worry that you've opened a can of worms, not knowing what to do. Understanding your anxiety is only the beginning. In the next chapter, you'll learn how to be more at peace by being compassionate with our anxiety and ourselves.

6

Acceptance and Self-Compassion

As a criminal lawyer, it was my job to represent clients at sentencing hearings. At a sentencing hearing, the crown attorney and I, the defense lawyer, each make a case for what sentence is appropriate for my client who has pled guilty or been found guilty. The judge, who decides the sentence, doesn't know much about my client aside from the facts and evidence against my client, making him look like a very bad person. The crown attorney often calls for the harshest punishment and argues that my client doesn't deserve mercy. The facts are that he committed a crime and caused other people suffering. Thus, he should pay for his actions.

Things look a lot different from my side. I know my client as a person. I know he likes to draw and read comic books. I know his mom is an alcoholic, and he was in and out of foster care. He's never met his dad. We chatted about his favorite places in the city. He's told me his hopes and dreams.

In the courtroom, I become my client's advocate. I truly believe in him. Despite his terrible mistake, I see his inherent goodness and potential. As I tell the court my client's story, I see the changing expressions, from disdain and disgust to hints of empathy and sadness for the unfortunate situation for all parties involved, including my client. My client is no longer the villain solely responsible for the tragedy. He's a person of worth deserving compassion and a second chance, as we all do.

What would it be like for you to be your own advocate, always believing in yourself and seeing the best, especially when you feel unworthy?

Nevertheless, it can feel hard, if not impossible, to be compassionate when it comes to ourselves. I remember how I once beat myself up for forgetting a deadline. I told myself how irresponsible I was, citing examples of my previous mistakes, that I didn't deserve to be a lawyer, and that no client should ever hire me because I could ruin their lives. Yet, I had no problem showing up every day advocating for my clients, urging the court to see the best in them who had committed domestic violence, robbery, drug trafficking, and so on. I was clearly being a hypocrite, applying a double standard.

Have you ever tried to practice self-compassion, only to revert to harsh self-talk when push came to shove? Why is it so hard to be kind to ourselves?

Here is an objection I hear from clients: "I'm just trying to make myself a better person. I'm giving myself tough love." The intention of tough love is often positive in that, at the end of the day, we want to improve ourselves. In practice, however, there is a fine line between tough love and bullying. People in high-pressure, fast-paced professions, such as nurses, lawyers, and doctors, often go through this scenario when they first enter the workforce. Their superiors and seniors often encourage them to sacrifice personal needs and work on little sleep, food, or even life outside of work. The rationale is, "It'll make you better at your job; I did the same when I was new too." They seem to forget that their juniors are *people*, not just nurses, lawyers, or doctors. Being better at work is only one aspect of their whole being. Are you perhaps also trying to advance one aspect of yourself and neglecting to see yourself as a person?

There is a lack of evidence that tough love approaches are effective. In fact, it can do more harm than good. For example, tough love treatment programs can make substance use disorder worse. There are now programs based on "communication, science, and connection," which can work better than those based on "isolation, judgment, and punishment" (Lodge, 2022).[11] If another approach that makes us feel good can work just as well as or even better than tough love, wouldn't we want to go with the

---

[11] Barbara Straus Lodge, "A Call for Kindness, Connection, and Science." *Journal of Substance Abuse Treatment* 141 (October 2022): 108839. https://doi.org/10.1016/j.jsat.2022.108839.

former? Why would we even want a feel-bad-now-in-order-to-maybe-feel-good-later approach?

Another objection I hear is that self-compassion is just "coddling" and spoiling ourselves. The common misconception is that we practice self-compassion by being okay with whatever we do or don't do (e.g., resting instead of studying or working, eating an extra donut because it makes me feel good, skipping a workout because I'm tired). Self-compassion is more nuanced than that, however. It's ultimately wanting what's best for us and helping us get there with an empathic, kind, and firm voice rather than being about what actions to approve or disapprove of.

My friend is a single mom, recently separated from her husband of 15 years. She has two young boys, the most precious people in the world to her. Being such a loving, dedicated mom came at a high cost, as she suffered from chronic anxiety. She couldn't help worrying about her sons, especially after the separation, which introduced big changes to her family.

It wasn't easy for her at first. For over a decade, she had conditioned herself to feel guilt, blame herself, and do whatever it took, including making personal sacrifices, to protect and nurture her kids. But with her therapist, she began to gradually explore and understand who she is as an individual and develop a relationship with that beautiful person inside. She learned to treat herself with kindness and compassion as she would treat her precious two boys. When she felt anxious, instead of piling on self-criticism and more worries, she comforted and encouraged herself that she was doing her best and that it was going to be okay. She has turned a corner and is living more than ever in the present rather than in anxiety about the future. She's doing it with gratitude and self-compassion, working through life's big and small issues one at a time.

Self-compassion doesn't make anxiety disappear, but it makes you stronger and more resilient. It prevents anxiety from escalating and makes anxiety much easier to cope with. Now it's your turn. If you'd like to experience these benefits, use the following process to practice self-compassion.

See Yourself as a Person

When we lack self-compassion, it's almost like we think of ourselves as a tool, not a person. We don't think about how our feelings might be hurt if we treat ourselves the way we do (e.g., *You should've done better. What's wrong with you? You are worthless.*) while we often take enormous care to protect other people's feelings and make them feel better with kind words (e.g., "You tried your best and can do better next time."). You are not a tool. You are a person with dignity, and you deserve to be treated by yourself as such.

Have you ever experienced road rage? Or perhaps you've heard of some crazy road rage stories where people were assaulted for merely cutting in? When we see other drivers misbehaving on the road, our minds often jump to the worst conclusions and assume they are horribly selfish and inconsiderate. This makes sense because we know nothing about the other driver as a person.

What, if anything, would change if we could somehow see their backgrounds and needs? The Uber driver who parked on the street, clearly marked as no stopping, could be a single dad supporting two children, rushing to finish his job and pick up the kids. While it may not excuse the inconsiderate behavior, would we not start to feel empathy for him instead of just seeing him as a nuisance? This is why you completed the exercises in the previous chapter. You also have reasons why you feel and do the things you do.

The Inner Child Exercise

Here is an exercise to help you start seeing and treating yourself as a person. It's often easier for us to be kind to helpless little ones who need our care (e.g., children, puppies). You can access the guided meditation for this exercise at facingyouranxiety.com.

Bring to mind a younger version of you, somewhere before the age of 12. Closing your eyes makes this exercise easier.

Think about what the child was going through at the time. What were the child's emotional needs? If you like, you can speak to the child and offer some words of kindness and wisdom like,

I'm here for you.

I'm so sorry you went through that.

It's okay for you to feel that way.

Understand, Accept, and Meet Your Needs

Being human means having needs, from basic needs such as food, sleep, and shelter to more complex needs like learning and growing. If you have a pet or have raised a child, you know what taking care of others' needs is like. You fed them when they were hungry (or to prevent them from being hungry), played with them to be happy, and expressed love through words, hugs, or actions so they feel loved.

You have needs too, and having needs doesn't mean you are broken or flawed in some way. Our job is not to correct ourselves by trying not to have needs. Our history is replete with tragic examples where people tried to "correct" others for being the way they naturally are, such as residential schools (Native American or Indigenous boarding schools) and conversion therapy. In many cultures, being left-handed was considered wrong, and children were forced to write and do things with their right hands, causing problems in their development and self-esteem. Let's not do the same thing to ourselves. It's okay and perfectly normal to have needs.

Like good parents, we need to know our needs and try our best to meet them. Here are some of our shared human needs:

- Need for physical comfort: feeling rested, hydrated, well-fed, warm, pain-free, etc.
- Need for safety and security: being physically and emotionally free from threats and danger
- Need for love and community: feeling connected to others
- Need for contribution and recognition: feeling like we (and what we do) matter and we are valued by others
- Need for learning and development: experiencing challenges and growth, expressing creativity

Our Shared Needs

Physical Comfort

Safety & Security

Love & Community

Contribution & Recognition

Learning & Development

It's ok to have needs

The psychologist Abraham Maslow portrayed these needs in a hierarchy (i.e., the need for physical comfort comes first before the need for love), but practically speaking, these needs often scream for our attention all at the same time.

Next time you don't feel well, instead of telling yourself to get over it like I used to, take some time to think about what you might be needing. Then, you can assure yourself that it's okay to have needs and think of some ways to get what you need. For example, feeling lonely is a sign that our need for love and community hasn't been met, and it might be a good time for us to schedule a dinner with friends or meet some new people. If we feel bored when everything in our lives is going great, instead of calling ourselves ungrateful, we can examine whether we have enough challenges to help us learn and grow. Like children, adults also need challenges to continue developing our physical, emotional, intellectual, and spiritual capacities. Practice listening to your needs and taking good care of yourself like a puppy or child. Be a loving, good caregiver.

See the Shared Suffering

When I was in law school, I thought I was the only one suffering from crippling anxiety and depression while everyone else was doing a great job coping with the pressure. This belief made me feel isolated, like I'm the only one who is weak and flawed. But in my three years there, two students committed suicide, and as a response, the school brought in various mental health initiatives, such as hiring an in-house therapist for law students and having massage days as well as 'bring your dogs to school' days to help students relax. Clearly, I wasn't the only one in pain.

When we feel like we are the only broken one, it's hard to have self-compassion. We feel like we don't deserve it and need to fix ourselves. It hurts. One thing I learned working as a therapist is that we *all* suffer, even those who look like they have it all. Insecurities, trauma, and pain are all part of what it means to be alive, and to exist in this world. We are not alone. You are not broken. You are human, just like all of us. When you feel isolated, remind yourself of this truth and help yourself feel more connected and understood.

Recognize the Self-Critical Voice

Learn to recognize the self-critical voice as it happens. One of the most powerful moments in therapy is when people realize how mean they have been to themselves. When I ask them to imagine speaking like that to their loved ones, they say, "I'd never say that to my son (sister, best friend, partner, etc.)!" Often, our self-critical voice lurks outside of our awareness. We start to feel horrible but don't realize we are doing that to ourselves.

Just because we have a thought doesn't mean that thought is true. Thoughts are merely mental events that occur in our minds. We are estimated to have over 6,000 thoughts per day.[12] Self-critical thoughts are not true and, what's worse, unhelpful. They make us feel worse about ourselves, bring down our mood and confidence, and interfere with relationships and performance.

Practice catching yourself whenever you have a self-critical thought. You may only catch it 10 percent of the time when you first start, and that's a good start. By doing this, we begin increasing our capacity to be more intentional with our thoughts. Don't worry about catching the thought and having to change it. That's too much work at this point. Simply notice the thought and label it as "thought." Thoughts come and go unless we hold on to them and make them stay, so just notice and let them come and go. We'll discuss more on this topic in the next chapter on mindfulness.

Learn Self-Compassion by Practicing Self-Compassion

People often say, "I don't know how to be kind to myself." But learning to be kind to ourselves is like learning how to walk. Babies don't sit around thinking, "I don't know how to walk, so I guess I'll just crawl until I learn how." Instead, they try to stand, fall, and try again, taking half a step before they fall again. Eventually, they start standing on their own and walking, and

---

[12] Julie Tseng and Jordan Poppenk, "Brain Meta-State Transitions Demarcate Thoughts across Task Contexts Exposing the Mental Noise of Trait Neuroticism." *Nature Communications* 11 (1): 3480 (2020). https://doi.org/10.1038/s41467-020-17255-9.

once that happens, there's no going back. Walking becomes as natural as breathing.

To learn self-compassion, start practicing what you learned in this chapter. Chances are you'll still be self-critical and dismissive of your needs from time to time. But the more you practice intentionally being compassionate to yourself, the easier and more natural it will become over time. There will come a time eventually when you'll be shocked whenever you are harsh to yourself because kindness to yourself would have become the norm. When that happens, you'll find it hard to be anxious for too long because you'll always have your inner advocate by your side, defending and rooting for you during tough times.

Easy Mindfulness

Between stimulus and response there is a space. In that
space is our power to choose our response. In our response
lies our growth and our freedom.

– Viktor E. Frankl

"You don't care about me! Why can't you, for once, try to understand me?" I shouted, my voice shaking with anger and pain. My friend, also shaken and hurt, retreated into her bedroom, slamming the door shut. I stood in the kitchen, feeling utterly alone and helpless.

What am I supposed to do now? This is too much. I wish all of this would just end. I can't do this anymore. Life is too much for me. I just can't.

I was sitting in the kitchen reeling from the pain when a thought popped in, *What exactly is this pain anyway?* It was a thought I had never had before, and it piqued my interest, even amid the intense emotional pain. I started to pay attention to my body to investigate. I felt a throbbing in my chest and a heavy feeling in my shoulders. I was genuinely curious, *What is this pain that's making me hurt so much?* Then, for a brief moment, the pain felt foreign to me. I became separate from the pain as if I was looking at it from the outside. At that moment, for the first time, I didn't feel the constant pain of depression. Or the urgency of anxiety to get rid of the pain immediately. I felt free. I could think clearly and felt my anger and pain magically subside.

Later I realized that this experience I had was called mindfulness. I had heard of the term before but never felt it firsthand like I did. I wanted to learn more about this amazing concept and how to recreate the experience to finally free myself from anxiety and depression. I bought books on mindfulness and signed up for an eight-week course. I took a deep dive and meditated daily for 30 minutes to one hour.

Unfortunately, my journey with mindfulness turned out to be frustrating. Although I gained a better understanding of mindfulness, I struggled to apply it when I needed it the most. Thanks to my eye-opening experience, I knew it was possible to detach myself from the constant pain of anxiety and depression. Nevertheless, I couldn't do it consciously for some reason. Mindfulness meditation was a hit or miss. Some days, I felt moments of freedom during my practice. On other days, I couldn't focus and felt worse at the end. And I got angry for wasting time and the little energy I had.

Have you ever felt frustrated from trying to meditate and not getting it right? The benefits of mindfulness are well-known but can be elusive for people who suffer from anxiety. Studies suggest that up to a quarter of people may experience adverse effects during mindfulness meditation, such as worsening symptoms of anxiety and depression (Farias and Wikholm, 2016[13]; Farias et al., 2020[14]; Schlosser et al., 2019[15]). I'm not trying to dissuade anyone from mindfulness meditation. Quite the opposite, mindfulness was central to my journey in freeing myself from anxiety, and I'd hate to see anyone toss mindfulness aside due to the same frustration I had.

Eventually, I gave up on using mindfulness to overcome my anxiety. That's when the door opened for me, and I finally got it. I was trying to use mindfulness as a weapon when it was meant to be a way of being. When I stopped being so intense and goal-oriented about mindfulness, I began to change. I became more patient and grounded. When I was triggered, I could observe my thoughts and feelings instead of immediately going into a state of panic. Mindfulness helped create a gap between my triggers and

---

[13] Miguel Farias and Catherine Wikholm, "Has the Science of Mindfulness Lost Its Mind?" *BJPsych Bulletin* 40 (6): 329–32 (December 2016). https://doi.org/10.1192/pb.bp.116.053686.

[14] Miguel Farias et al.,"Adverse Events in Meditation Practices and Meditation-Based Therapies: A Systematic Review." *Acta Psychiatrica Scandinavica* 142 (5): 374-393 (August 2020). https://doi.org/10.1111/acps.13225.

[15] Marco Schlosser et al., "Unpleasant Meditation-Related Experiences in Regular Meditators: Prevalence, Predictors, and Conceptual Considerations." *PLOS ONE* 14 (5): e0216643 (2019). https://doi.org/10.1371/journal.pone.0216643.

responses to the triggers. More and more often, I was able to choose my thoughts and actions to help myself and the situation instead of making it worse. I began to live more and more in the present rather than the pain of the past or the anxiety of the future.

Learning mindfulness doesn't have to involve hours of meditation (although it helps). With the right mindset and intention, you can begin to adopt mindfulness as a way of life rather than it becoming another tool that fails to fix your anxiety. Here are some mistakes to avoid and simple practices to easily make mindfulness how you live instead of what you do.

Mistake #1: Not being focused during meditation means nothing came out of it.

This mistaken assumption made me dread sitting down to meditate and left me frustrated after the practice. Like many anxiety-driven Type A people, I despise wasting time and not getting results. I also hate not being good at what I do. I thought I sucked at meditation because I felt distracted 90 percent of the time (70 percent on good days). Every time I meditated, I felt discouraged and less motivated to do it again. This made me see meditation as a chore at best and torture at worst. This attitude negatively affected what happened during my meditation practice. We tend to get what we expect (i.e., expecting I'm going to have a terrible time meditating leads me to have a terrible time during meditation).

To escape this cycle, I needed to shift my mindset. I learned that during mindfulness meditation, we are supposed to get distracted. The point of mindfulness meditation is not to stay focused on your breath, sounds, sensations, etc. It is to *practice intentionally bringing our attention back to our choice of focus* repeatedly to train our minds. Therefore, the more you get distracted, the more opportunities you have to train your mind and the more "work" you get done during your meditation. With this mindset, staying in the present and being non-judgmental when our minds wander becomes easier. In those moments of distraction, we can *notice and choose* to bring our attention back to what we want to focus on instead, for example, our breath. This practice is what strengthens our ability to stay grounded when we are at risk of being taken over by anxiety. Imagine being able to simply notice your anxious thoughts and feelings and *choose* to shift your focus to more helpful, calm thoughts. Training in mindfulness allows you to do that, gradually but surely.

Mistake #2: Mindfulness meditation is supposed to make me feel better.

When I started to meditate regularly and had a bad experience, I felt misled and let down. If the books and teachers say such great things about mindfulness, why is it making me feel worse? This expectation almost made me give up on mindfulness because "it wasn't working."

Re-examining and adjusting this expectation can help make our mindfulness practice easier. Yes, mindfulness can definitely help us feel better over time. But it's often not an effective short-term solution to acute emotional crises. If your purpose in mindfulness meditation is just to feel better in the moment, there are better alternatives, which I'll share in later chapters. Mindfulness meditation is more like a workout than a pill. Doing it can sometimes be painful in the moment but leads to long-term resilience.

Mistake #3: I must push through regardless of how I'm feeling.

As mentioned above, mindfulness meditation can sometimes be painful and make us feel worse. It's important to be gentle to ourselves. In my experience, it doesn't help to be a mindfulness meditation warrior, willing to tough it out and get it done at whatever cost. Discipline is important but not everything. Even when we physically work out, we must pace ourselves or risk picking up an injury and slowing our progress. Listen to your mind and body and adjust your practice as necessary. If doing a breath meditation for 20 minutes felt arduous and not fun at all, it's okay to do a different mindfulness practice for a shorter period of time, such as walking meditation for ten minutes.

This is the central lesson in all three mistakes: let go of the need to achieve through mindfulness. It makes it unnecessarily hard and boring. Developing mindfulness is like learning a healthy new habit. Make it as easy and pleasant as possible so you'll enjoy learning and practicing mindfulness until, eventually, it becomes second nature, like breathing and walking. To help you with that, here are some practices you can start immediately with minimal discomfort and resistance.

Unconventional Mindfulness Practices

Micro-Moment Mindfulness

The easiest way to start developing mindfulness is to work it into your daily routine. Mindfulness is about being fully in the present moment, and we are often on autopilot throughout the day. Where is your mind usually at while brushing your teeth? Probably anywhere but in the present moment, as our minds are used to thinking about the past or the future. Perhaps you are busy thinking about the day ahead, how tired you are, or something that happened on the previous day. This is normal and a great opportunity to practice mindfulness.

When you go about brushing your teeth, cooking, eating, walking, driving, or doing any other usual activities, practice intentionally noticing the present moment. The easiest way to do this is to engage your senses: seeing, hearing, touching, smelling, and tasting. For example, you can focus on how the toothbrush feels on your teeth and gum and the fresh scent of the toothpaste. You can feel the water massaging the inside of your mouth as you gargle and rinse. When walking and thinking, you can practice bringing your attention back to the present by noticing different colors in your surroundings and the sensations on your feet as you take each step. And you don't need to do this continuously all the time to benefit from this exercise. Even a few times a day can help you build your mindfulness muscle and develop an awareness of the present.

Mini Meditation

Although meditation is an important practice in cultivating mindfulness, long meditation sessions can feel daunting and discouraging for people not used to it. Instead of starting with 30-minute or even 10-minute sessions, start small and work up to longer sessions. If you were a beginner in weightlifting, you wouldn't start by trying to bench press 250 lbs, would you? Meditation is the mental equivalent of weightlifting. If you want to get better at it, you need to build your mental muscle gradually and work your way up to longer, more focused sessions, experiencing success along the way, like how you would incrementally increase the lifting weight from 50 lbs to 70 lbs to 100 lbs, etc. Trying to do too much at once can hinder your progress.

Start by doing this one-minute meditation at least once a day. Set a timer for one minute, close your eyes, and pay attention to your breath. When you get distracted by a thought, sound, or something else, simply label it (e.g., "thought," "sound," "sensation") and bring your attention back to your breath. When your timer goes off, you can go back to your day. It's easy and takes no time. My clients love doing this mini meditation and say they feel better, more grounded, and ready to tackle the rest of their day. If and when you feel ready, you can increase the time to two minutes, three minutes, five minutes, etc. There is also nothing wrong with keeping it at one minute, as it's already many times better than no meditation at all. If you prefer a guided meditation, you can download a three-minute breathing meditation at facingyouranxiety.com.

Thought Bubbles/Movie Screen

This practice is especially good for learning to stay centered and grounded when emotionally triggered. When we are anxious, we often get sucked into thoughts or stories we make up (e.g., *Why did I do that? He must think I'm stupid and awkward now. I hate myself*). Thoughts are mental events in our minds and are not necessarily true. If we develop an ability to see our thoughts as an outside observer, we can discern and choose whether or not to engage in those thoughts. The ability to let go of unhelpful thoughts is fundamental to freeing yourself from anxiety.

Next time you struggle with difficult thoughts, such as obsessing over your mistakes or worries, try this exercise. First, find a quiet place where you won't be interrupted and close your eyes. Start noticing your thoughts. Imagine seeing your thoughts inside thought bubbles like those in comic books. If it helps, you can say to yourself, *I'm having a thought that [insert your thought].*

Alternatively, you can imagine yourself in a movie theatre and see your thoughts appearing and disappearing from the screen in front of you. Notice what it's like to be an observer of your thoughts.

Being with Your Feelings

This practice is similar to the above exercise except that we work with feelings. Like how we can get sucked into our own thoughts, it can be easy for us to get taken over by strong emotions. Similar to thoughts, feelings come and go throughout the day. When I was anxious, I often unknowingly prolonged the very feelings I didn't want by thinking obsessively about them. Feeling anxious meant that I'd have thoughts like *What if I mess up? What if I have a miserable time? I hate feeling this way. Why do I keep feeling anxious?* Being anxious about being anxious is a theme that many anxiety sufferers struggle with, and mindfulness provides a solution.

We can learn to observe our feelings, just as we can with our thoughts, and let them do their thing before they leave our system. No painful feeling is permanent unless we keep it going by resisting or avoiding it. When you notice an intense feeling that begins to take over, pay attention to how it feels in your body. Scan your body from head to toe, noticing the sensations. For example, when you feel angry, you may notice tension in your head, heat in your face, and tightness in your shoulders and chest. Be curious to know what happens in your body, observe the sensations, and be with them during this practice. It's okay to have those sensations. Take a few deep, slow breaths as you continue your observation.

These four mini-mindfulness practices may not seem like much on their own, but they add up over time. My client Nora was incredulous when she experienced the power of simply being with feelings. Having struggled with anxiety and intense emotions most of her life, she found it challenging to make good use of traditional mindfulness practices. When she started integrating these easy practices into her life, she immediately noticed the benefits. Soon after, she reported having a breakthrough. She realized that she didn't have to be afraid of her feelings anymore because when she started to simply be with them, they just went away on their own. Experiencing anxiety as a passing feeling empowered Nora to push herself beyond her comfort zone. She felt free to be true to herself and start pursuing her dreams because now she knew she could successfully cope when difficulties arose in life.

8

Unlearning Your Anxiety Habits

Emily suffers from chronic anxiety and claustrophobia. It started when she was accidentally trapped in a storage room a few years ago. When she started seeing me, the fear had generalized and taken over other areas of her life. She struggled with a fear so overwhelming that she had trouble riding the subway, buses, airplanes, and elevators, as well as being in public without an "escape plan."

As usual, the initial focus was to help Emily get to know, appreciate, and be kind to herself. It's always interesting that the amazing character and strengths that jump out immediately to me are almost invisible to my clients. Emily is a very kind, caring, and strong person who has overcome many adversities in life. She uses her gift of empathy to help people as an occupational therapist. But to herself, she felt like a weak and fragile person who is unable to cope with difficulties. As she learned to see the past significant events through the lens of empowerment rather than as a victim, she began to feel more confident and resilient. She also started to develop mindfulness with the help of the mini-practices and learned that thoughts and feelings are not absolute truths.

Despite the overall improvement, Emily couldn't help but notice that she continued to struggle with anxiety every day as if it was background noise. I asked her to describe when she usually starts feeling anxious and what typically happens in her mind.

"Well, it's like I'm constantly anxious, but I notice it, especially if I'm going somewhere. I think about having to take an elevator, and it makes me think about all the ways it can go wrong. I try not to visit people who live in high-rise condos. What if I'm trapped in the elevator and I can't breathe? What if there's another person with me in the elevator and I start panicking? What if I can't take the elevator and I have to walk up 30 flights of stairs? I don't want to arrive sweaty and exhausted."

"Ok, let's pause here and consider what you've been doing. Chronic anxiety is often driven by our own mental habits. In other words, we are making ourselves anxious by doing certain things over and over again without realizing we are doing it."

"You mean I've been doing this to myself? What do you mean?"

We've discussed that there is nothing wrong with feeling anxious from time to time. It's meant to protect us from environmental threats and help us be more prepared. Nevertheless, we've established in Chapter 4 that chronic anxiety is harmful and there is no good reason why anyone should live in that state. Chronic anxiety is a self-perpetuating cycle, and it goes like this. We feel anxious, so we avoid, worry, or think about -case scenarios, making us even more anxious. The more anxious we feel, the more likely we will avoid, worry, and plan for the worst case. And on and on. To break the cycle of chronic anxiety, we must become aware of and stop engaging in these four mental habits that fuel the cycle: avoiding, worrying, what-if-ing, and catastrophizing.

Using her mindfulness skills, Emily started to catch herself every time she engaged in one of the four habits. She was surprised to find out just how much time she spent avoiding, worrying, what-if-ing, and catastrophizing. In fact, she realized that whenever she was alone with her thoughts, she somehow made herself anxious. She decided that it was time to stop. She was determined to help herself escape the cycle of chronic anxiety. Even though it wasn't easy at first, she began to unlearn the habits by noticing, consciously stopping herself, and instead doing the exercises I taught her. One day, she realized that her mind no longer automatically catastrophizes but could look at both the upside and the downside. She learned that if she could imagine failures and disasters, she could also imagine successes and good fortune.

How often do you avoid, worry, think of what-ifs, or catastrophize due to anxiety? Would you continue to engage in these habits if you knew that doing so was making you more anxious and trapped in the cycle of chronic anxiety? You might say, "Okay, I get it, but easier said than done." And that's fair, which is why I'll show you exactly how to break these habits and retrain your mind. I'll review each of these habits and explain why they're harmful, how to stop, and what to do instead.

Avoiding

Why It Hurts

On its face, avoiding seems the easiest way to stop feeling anxious. Don't like public speaking? No problem. Just eliminate it from your life or minimize it. That birthday party you've been dreading? Just make up an excuse and don't go. But is it really this easy? You probably already know intuitively that we can't avoid our way out of anxiety. On a practical level, avoiding creates other issues. For instance, eliminating public speaking from your life may limit your career opportunities and keep you stuck at a low-level job. And if you skip that birthday party, your friend may feel disappointed and hurt, negatively affecting your relationship. You could've also had an amazing time at the party and met some cool people, but you'd never know because you were never there.

If you want to overcome anxiety, avoiding really hurts your chance because it takes away opportunities for you to learn and build confidence. Avoiding something that triggers anxiety consciously and subconsciously reinforces the message "I can't handle it." This not only limits your life but also hurts your confidence. When our confidence is down, the list of the things we feel anxious about and avoid can only grow.

How to Stop Avoiding

Set an intention.

Ask yourself: *What's more important than avoiding this thing that's causing discomfort?*

Your intention can be on a high level or more immediate. For example, if you are trying to avoid meeting your significant other's family, your immediate intention might be *I love my partner and care about supporting my partner.* At the same time, your overarching intention for this and all other challenges might be *I want to be the person who is authentic and radiates self-assurance.*

Remind yourself of your intention whenever you catch yourself avoiding or are tempted to avoid. It helps to write it down and display it where you can see it often or memorize it and repeat it like a mantra.

What to Do Instead of Avoiding: Exposure

A great way to neutralize any fear is becoming familiar with the feared stimulus, which is why exposure therapy is widely used to treat anxiety disorders. Exposure therapy involves deliberately confronting your fears in a structured manner. For example, if you are afraid of dogs, exposure may involve being in a room with a leashed friendly dog and eventually petting a dog. Instead of avoiding, you can facilitate exposure therapy for yourself to gradually neutralize your triggers to anxiety.

Let's take a look at an example. Maureen suffers from social anxiety, which has kept her trapped at home with minimal interactions with others. First, we take some time to think about why overcoming social anxiety is important to her. She recalls her desire to visit her friend who moved to Switzerland. She thinks about how nice it would be to see her dear friend and explore the beautiful country (she loves mountains). But as things stand, it feels impossible for her to travel to a foreign country as she is terrified of talking to strangers. She decides to take baby steps and start neutralizing fears through exposure. Every morning, she takes her dog out for a walk and makes it a task to talk to one other person, however short the conversation might be. She then rewards herself with encouraging words whenever she faces her fear (*Yes, I did it! It's a step in the right direction. This will all add up.*). Then, she moves on to an activity that makes her more anxious, like asking a stranger for directions. It feels very uncomfortable at first, but it starts to get better as she intentionally repeats the same behavior. Her next tasks might be taking the subway, having a 10-minute conversation with an acquaintance, and going to a restaurant alone.

If you suffer from anxiety that's not as crippling as Maureen's, you can feel free to take bolder action. If you fear public speaking, why not sign up for Toastmasters or an improv class? If you are afraid of dating or rejections, you can desensitize yourself by deliberately getting rejected, like Jia Jiang, who set out to get rejected 100 times and gave a TED talk about it.[16]

Worrying

Why It Hurts

Worrying appears to be a natural by-product or consequence of anxiety. When we are anxious, we tend to worry, meaning our minds are focused on the trouble or the problem in ways that scare, upset, or make us unhappy. Worrying about money provides a good example. Have you ever worried about not having enough? Perhaps there was a time in your life you had a lot of upcoming or unpaid bills and/or a reduction in income due to circumstances out of your control. These may have been the thoughts occupying your mind:

> *Will I have enough money to pay for rent/mortgage? At this rate, I don't know if I'll have to go into debt. My savings will run out soon. It's so hard to find a job these days, and I haven't had any offers for interviews in a while. I don't have time. I'm running out of time. It will be so embarrassing if I have to move back in with my parents. Everyone will think I'm a failure.*

---

[16] Jia Jiang, *Rejection Proof: How I Beat Fear and Became Invincible Through 100 Days of Rejection* (New York: Harmony, 2015).

As you read the above paragraph, how do you feel? Probably more anxious and maybe a bit hopeless. Worrying cheers up and motivates no one. Worrying is often our effort to problem-solve our way out of undesirable situations. But it does not help because it drains us and can overwhelm us with anxiety, leading to paralysis. There is a better way to problem-solve than worrying.

How to Stop Worrying

When you find yourself worrying obsessively about something, simply become aware, pause, and label it either silently or aloud, "worrying." Then, set aside some time to sit with your thoughts as an observer instead of actively engaging with your thoughts. Use the thought bubbles/movie screen technique from Chapter 7. See your thoughts popping in and out of your awareness. Let them come and go. This will help you separate yourself from your thoughts and gain some distance from your worries so you can start taking effective action.

What to Do Instead of Worrying

You can effectively transform worrying into actions through the following steps.

First, write down what you are worried about (e.g., I'm worried my boss doesn't like me).

Next, ask yourself, *(1) "Is it within my control or outside of my control?"*

Although it may feel like everything is or should be within your control, try to be fair and objective here. For example, if you are worried about your boss's opinion of you, is it really within your control whether or not you impress your boss? You can improve the quality of your work, but at the end of the day, your boss may not be so impressed because she could be having a bad day or has unrealistically high expectations.

If it is outside your control, ask yourself does it help that I'm thinking and stressing about this? If the answer is "Yes, it does help," it indicates it's within your control, so move on to the next question. If the answer is "No, it does NOT help," then you need to help yourself and let it go.

If it appears that it is truly within your control, move on to the next question.

(2) Is it my problem or someone else's problem?

If you say it's my problem, it's time to make a plan of action: what steps or actions can I take to improve it? Being stressed about something isn't necessarily bad in and of its own. It could be a signal that something needs to be done about it. If you are stressed about your toddler getting hurt around the house, the right thing to do may not be to just let it go. The better thing to do would be to baby-proof the house, install baby gates, and remove dangerous objects to ensure your child is safe.

If it's "NOT my problem but someone else's problem," ask yourself, "Do I really want to keep stressing about this when I've got problems of my own?"

Ultimately, other people's problems are not within our control. We can give them all the right tools and advice, but we can't make them do what we think is good for them. As the saying goes, we can lead a horse to water but can't make it drink. Do yourself a favor and let go of stressing about someone else's problem.

EXAMPLES

Example #1

"I'm stressed that my colleagues think I'm stupid and incompetent."

Is it within my control? No, I can't control how my colleagues think of me.

LET IT GO.

Example #2

"I'm worried about my parents' relationship."

Is it within my control? I don't know, but maybe I should intervene (which makes it within my control).

Is it my problem? No, it's really their problem, and they'll likely fall into the same patterns even after I intervene. LET IT GO.

Example #3

"I'm stressed about the upcoming presentation at work. Public speaking stresses me out."

Is it within my control? Yes.

Is it my problem? Yes.

What steps/actions can I take to make it better?

- schedule three hours to study the subject more and prepare well
- watch YouTube videos for tips on public speaking
- speak to my mentor/coach/colleague at work for advice

"What-If-Ing" and Catastrophizing

Why It Hurts

What-if-ing is thinking of or creating bad scenarios in your mind (e.g., What if I make a mistake and get fired? What if I get a panic attack?), and catastrophizing is assuming that the worst will happen (e.g., He hasn't texted me back in two hours, so it must mean that I'm being ghosted.). They are both harmful for the same reason and share the same antidote.

We humans are imaginative by nature. And we love stories. As you may remember from the previous chapters, our brains are not good at distinguishing between imagined and real events. This means that when you imagine a worst-case scenario, it's as if you are already living it, resulting in the same physiological and emotional responses (Reddan, Wager & Schiller, 2018).[17] This is how you can make yourself anxious by continuing to imagine, and thereby living, unwanted and scary events that may or may not happen.

Do you ever watch horror or thriller movies? If you've ever watched one (and if the movie was reasonably decent), you probably remember feeling anxious, scared, or stressed during some parts of the movie, even though, consciously, you knew that you weren't actually being chased by a serial killer or haunted by an evil spirit. You may have also had some physical reactions while watching it: sweaty palms, heart racing, and tightness. At the movie's end, the lights came on, and you got to return to your life. The movie was just a story. But what if (no pun intended) you were a character in the movie and that was your life and world? Or what if someone forced you to watch horror movie after horror movie non-stop? That wouldn't be entertaining

---

[17] Marianne Cumella Reddan, Tor Dessart Wager, and Daniela Schiller, "Attenuating Neural Threat Expression with Imagination." *Neuron* 100 (4): 994-1005.e4 (2018). https://doi.org/10.1016/j.neuron.2018.10.047.

anymore, would it? Constantly creating what-ifs and catastrophizing is like being stuck in a horror movie and nightmare scenarios where everything goes wrong. The good news is you can choose to walk out and stop watching the horror movie of your making. You can even choose to watch something more lighthearted and cheerful instead.

How to Stop What-If-Ing and Catastrophizing

At this point, you may object by saying that thinking about the what-ifs helps you prepare for whatever may come along and prevent disasters. As a lawyer, my job was to prepare for trials to the best of my ability by trying to anticipate everything that could go wrong. I was pretty good at this. However, the problem started when I applied this to my life. Unlike trials, life has no boundaries. Trials are about isolated cases, and they finish at some point.

In contrast, in life, we are always going through different events and circumstances which happen at the same time, one after the other, and this continues until the day we die. Trying to anticipate everything that could go wrong in everything that was happening in my life was exhausting and made me a very unhappy, chronically anxious person. I'm saying that there is a time and place for preparation. If the event is truly important to you, you can set aside time to think critically and objectively about how best to prepare for it, including risk factors. Thinking all the time about what can go wrong hurts your quality of life and prevents you from thinking clearly as you'd be thinking from an anxious place.

The key to overcoming what-if-ing and catastrophizing is to become aware. What-if-ing is a habit. To break a habit, it takes awareness and consistent response. Make it a game to catch yourself every time you think *what if*. It's a game of mindfulness. When you catch yourself, pause the thought in its track, label it ("what-if-ing"), and bring your attention back to the present using your senses (e.g., notice what you are seeing, touching, hearing, etc.). You don't have to reason and convince yourself why the what-if scenario is wrong and likely will never happen. If you try to reason with your thoughts, you'll fall into the trap of trying to think your way out of anxiety, which never works. Simply notice the what-if thought and bring your attention to the present without engaging. By doing this, you'll not only prevent what-if-ing from making you anxious but also regain control over your thinking and mood.

What to Do Instead of What-If-Ing and Catastrophizing

Since our brains treat imagined events as real, we can use this to our advantage. Instead of thinking of what-if scenarios you don't want, think about what you want to see happen. For example, if you have an upcoming presentation, you may have been used to thinking about scenarios such as what if I freeze? What if I stutter? What if someone asks me a question I can't answer? And so on. First, prepare to the best of your ability. Then, use your mind to help yourself perform even better. Many elite athletes use visualization to prepare for their competition because they understand that the mental game is just as important. When they train their minds this way, they visualize success: e.g., making a perfect shot, executing the swing with a beautiful form, and knocking the ball out of the park. They don't visualize dropping the ball or missing the shot. Likewise, you can also think about (or even visualize) the good what-ifs. Think about the outcomes you desire and what it would be like to achieve them. For the presentation scenario, it might be as follows: *I'm standing tall, making my points succinctly with authority, and connecting with my audience. I feel excitement and a sense of achievement. I'm improving each time I speak in public.*

Catch Yourself

Catch yourself and stop engaging in avoiding, worrying, what-if-ing, and catastrophizing, and you'll quickly notice how much lighter you feel on a day-to-day basis. I've prepared a cheat sheet for you so you can easily remember and apply what you've learned in this chapter. You can download the cheat sheet at facingyouranxiety.com.

9

Leveraging Mind-Body Connection

When was the last time you felt relaxed? I mean truly relaxed. This might be a hard question to answer if you suffer from anxiety. When I ask my clients this question, they are often stumped. After a few moments of searching their memories, they may say, "When I was on vacation six months ago." Sometimes people answer "never" and "I don't know how to relax." What about you? How often, if ever, do you feel relaxed?

The stress arising from the busy, modern lifestyle makes it incredibly hard for us to rest and regularly feel relaxed if left to our natural tendencies. In the face of a threat, our bodies have a built-in alarm system called fight-or-flight. Whereas in the past, the system was triggered when we were literally in life-or-death situations (e.g., running into a tiger). In this day and age, we face threats everywhere, albeit typically not life-threatening. It starts at a young age. According to a 2019 Pew Research Centre report, 70 percent of teens reported that anxiety and depression are major problems for them. Of those surveyed, 61 percent reported that they "feel a lot of pressure to get good grades."[18] Think about it. How many deadlines have you had when you were a student? When one assignment or test finishes, you just get another one, and this continues for however many years you are in school, around 20 years if you pursue advanced degrees. You may have experienced a fluctuating sense of self-worth depending on your grade, rewards, and punishments from authority figures. Since we were young, we've faced constant pressure to perform and anxiety as a result. Some of my clients even told me their schools ranked students and posted the results on bulletin boards with their full names for everyone to see. Is it even a surprise that they struggle with performance anxiety now as adults?

Another stress factor as humans is our desire to fit in. The possibility of social rejection is a threat. It was a life-or-death threat back when being kicked out from your tribe meant death in the wild, and we still experience it as a threat. The problem is that in modern life, the possibility of social rejection is everywhere and happens all the time. Do you use social media? I probably don't need to remind you of how many times you felt bad while on social media. Do you use your cell phone for texting or messaging apps? I wonder if you've ever felt hurt that someone didn't message you back quickly or worried that you hurt someone's feelings by not replying quickly enough. Or perhaps you didn't like the tone of the message and were left wondering if they were mad at you. All of this is stress that can trigger fight or

---

[18] Pew Research Center, *Most U.S. Teens See Anxiety and Depression as a Major Problem Among Their Peers*, (February 2019).

flight. And lastly, if we need an extra dose of anxiety, we only need to turn on the news channel or open our news app. There are terrible threats all over the world, like wars, climate change, sky-high inflation, and crime.

All this to say, in this day and age, it's easy to spend too much time being anxious and not enough time being relaxed and calm. We are off balance. The result is chronic anxiety where our minds and bodies are constantly tense and living in threat. As we discussed in Chapter 4, the more frequently we feel anxious, the easier it becomes for us to stay that way and feel triggered next time. To free ourselves from chronic anxiety, we need to actively break this cycle by consciously guiding ourselves into relaxation.

Let's consider this in terms of our physiology. Our bodily functions are regulated by the autonomic nervous system, which has two divisions: the sympathetic nervous system and the parasympathetic nervous system. The sympathetic system's priority is short-term survival, so it is activated when we encounter a threat. It gets us ready for action and keeps us sharp. It's commonly referred to as the "fight-or-flight" response.

In contrast, the parasympathetic system is for keeping our bodies in harmony and is designed for long-term health. It relaxes our bodies and triggers the "rest-and-digest" response. Each of the two systems becomes dominant at different times. When you have a deadline approaching and you haven't finished the work you are supposed to submit, you may have noticed some changes in your body that are markedly different from when you are reading and sipping a drink at a beach. That's your sympathetic and parasympathetic systems at work.

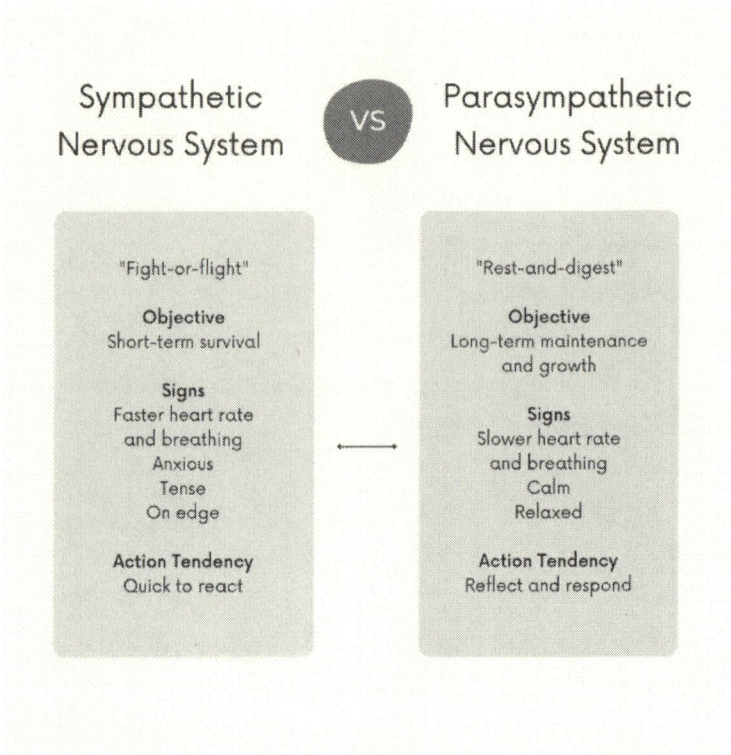

Sympathetic Nervous System — VS — Parasympathetic Nervous System

Sympathetic Nervous System	Parasympathetic Nervous System
"Fight-or-flight"	"Rest-and-digest"
Objective Short-term survival	**Objective** Long-term maintenance and growth
Signs Faster heart rate and breathing Anxious Tense On edge	**Signs** Slower heart rate and breathing Calm Relaxed
Action Tendency Quick to react	**Action Tendency** Reflect and respond

I was a stressed-out lawyer overwhelmed with deadlines, uncertainties, and angry people around me, and I was one of the people who didn't know how to relax. I knew I felt better when I exercised, but I quickly returned to feeling stressed when the activity ended. Because I didn't know other ways to relax, I exercised like a fanatic seven days a week. I wasn't getting any long-term improvement in anxiety, but at least it kept me from being tipped over the edge into a meltdown. When exercising wasn't available to me, sometimes I self-medicated with alcohol because I noticed it helped my body relax (could this be why one in five lawyers are "problem drinkers"?[19]). After all, no one ever taught me that I needed to relax or how to do it.

My life looks different now. Because my default state is calm awareness, I notice quickly when I start feeling tense and anxious. I'm in tune with my body, so when my fight-or-flight system is activated, I know how to work with my body to bring myself back to a balanced state. I exercise for fun rather than relying on it to sustain me. I can cope with a wide variety of stressors in my life (e.g., relationship issues, financial burdens, life changes like moving, and problems at work) because my body isn't constantly doused with stress hormones and therefore depleted. Most days, I have more than enough fuel to keep me going, and I know when to prioritize rest and recharge instead of pushing through at whatever cost. And I never have to turn to alcohol for stress-relief.

Getting to this place required learning to work with my body, rather than fighting against it, by doing the following:

1. Find a rhythm of stress and rest/relaxation

---

[19] Patrick R. Krill, Ryan Johnson, and Linda Albert, "The Prevalence of Substance Use and Other Mental Health Concerns among American Attorneys." *Journal of Addiction Medicine* 10 (1): 46–52 (2016). https://doi.org/10.1097/adm.0000000000000182.

2. Recognize when you are in fight-or-flight and let go of the urge to resist

3. Use breathing techniques to activate the parasympathetic nervous system

4. Find your rest and relaxation and do it regularly

Find a Rhythm of Stress and Rest/Relaxation

I was obsessed with bettering myself, whether in my career or even in hobbies and never liked to rest. Perhaps you struggle with the idea of rest and relaxation too. We live in a hustle culture and are often told "no pain, no gain." Yes, we do have to face and endure some pain to achieve growth. But do you know when it is too much pain, at which point it becomes unproductive in achieving your desired outcome? It's like when we do strength training with weights. We lift weights which stresses and damages our muscle fibers so they can rebuild and get bigger. But if we push too much past our current capacity by overdoing it, it results in injuries like tendonitis and pulled muscles that take us out for weeks and months. What's more, muscle growth happens while you rest, not while you are lifting weights.

It works the same way in overcoming chronic anxiety by becoming more resilient. We need to find our rhythm of stress and relaxation. A mentally stressful activity strains our bodies, just like when we exercise or engage in hard physical labor. It doesn't mean that we stop doing what makes us feel stressed, such as going to work and being in a relationship, because stress is necessary for us to function and grow. Instead, we learn to recognize when we are overdoing it and need to rest, relax, and recover. Then, we go back to our stressors. We realize that we can do a bit more, a bit better when we are healthy, so we push ourselves a bit more until we know it's time to rest again. We do this repeatedly, and sooner or later, we realize that our capacity has expanded. This is how we build resilience.

I want to emphasize that both stress and rest/relaxation are necessary, not one or the other. There was a time I felt so overwhelmed with anxiety and depression that I stopped functioning for a while. So did my clients who had to take extended leaves from work. If this is your situation, please know that this is okay. It doesn't mean you are broken. We are not designed to just push through massive amounts of stress day after day without relief. Sooner or later, our bodies will send a strong signal that we need breaks through physical and mental illnesses. What's important is what happens now. You might be afraid you'll never return to the person you were, as I was. You may be thinking, "What if I can never go back to work?" The truth is that, no, you will not go back to the person you were. That was unsustainable. You'll build yourself back up, one brick at a time, into a stronger, better version of yourself. One way to build a strong foundation is to find your rhythm of stress and rest/relaxation. Think of yourself in rehab. You don't give up walking because it hurts. You start walking, feel pain, rest, and go at it again. Controlled stress is good, and rest is good.

Recognize Fight-or-Flight

Working with our bodies starts with listening to our bodies. Many of us are conditioned to live our whole lives in our heads, meaning we are constantly thinking and generally not paying attention to what's happening in our bodies. How do you know when you are anxious? Think about it. Is it because you start having racing thoughts with a tone of anxiety? Do you have a myriad of physical symptoms, such as sweaty palms, heart palpitations, and tremors? Perhaps all at the same time? Whatever your specific symptoms might be, half the battle is in learning to recognize as quickly as possible that your sympathetic nervous system has been activated and you are now in a fight-or-flight response. As soon as you start noticing the familiar signs of anxiety, say to yourself, "fight-or-flight." Labeling your anxiety this way tends to take the edge off the alarm. Feeling anxious is not an emergency in and of itself unless there's an actual emergency, such as fire, robbery, etc., to which you must quickly respond. Most often, it's just our body reacting to what we perceive as a threat, like anticipating our boss being angry or family being disappointed in us, whether or not it's an accurate assessment of the situation.

You'll likely experience an urge to think yourself out of anxiety. *This can't be happening! I don't want to feel this way. I need to get out of here, etc.* This is a trap. Stop resisting the natural activation of your nervous system. It doesn't help. Simply label it as "fight-

or-flight." And move on to the next step of using the skills and techniques shared in this book to help yourself.

Activate the Rest-and-Digest

Do you ever get annoyed when you are really worked up and someone tells you to take a deep breath? I used to think it was ridiculous to try to breathe away anxiety. But I was wrong. Breathing techniques are based in science and work wonders in regulating our nervous system. If it's perceiving threats that activates fight-or-flight (sympathetic nervous system), slow deep breathing can counteract this and activate rest-and-digest (parasympathetic nervous system), letting your body know that it's safe.

The best way to use deep breathing to retrain your chronically anxious body-mind is to practice regularly, not just when triggered. In other words, practicing deep breathing is more like taking vitamins rather than applying a bandage. If you intend to free yourself from chronic anxiety, deep breathing is not meant to be used like a painkiller, although it tends to have that effect. By practicing deep breathing regularly, you'll teach your body-mind the difference between tension/stress and relaxation and that feeling good and relaxed is safe and desirable. The more you experience the feeling of relaxation, the easier it will become for you to return to that state (remember neuroplasticity from earlier). Try the following breathing techniques and feel the effect for yourself. You'll notice what it's like to be in rest-and-digest, in contrast to fight-or-flight.

4-6 Deep Breathing

This easy breathing technique can be done anywhere, anytime. Find a comfortable posture; your legs uncrossed if you are sitting. Take a slow deep breath in for four seconds. Then, extend your out breath, breathing out very slowly for six seconds.

Count 1-2-3-4 slowly as you breathe in and 1-2-3-4-5-6 as you breathe out.

How does it feel? Most people feel relaxed and find it calming to focus on their breath, quieting their anxious thoughts.

Practice 4-6 Deep Breathing three times a day for about a minute, at random or certain times such as after waking up, lunchtime, and before bedtime. If it helps, set a reminder on your smartphone.

Cardiac Coherence

This is a therapeutic breathing practice developed by Dr. David O'Hare. As illustrated below, when we are stressed and anxious (i.e., in fight-or-flight), our heart rate becomes incoherent. Have you ever noticed your heart beating fast and all over the place when you are anxious or upset? As deep breathing slows down our heart rate and stimulates the vagus nerve (thus the parasympathetic nervous system), Cardiac coherence aims to bring our heart rate into rhythmic, coherent patterns.

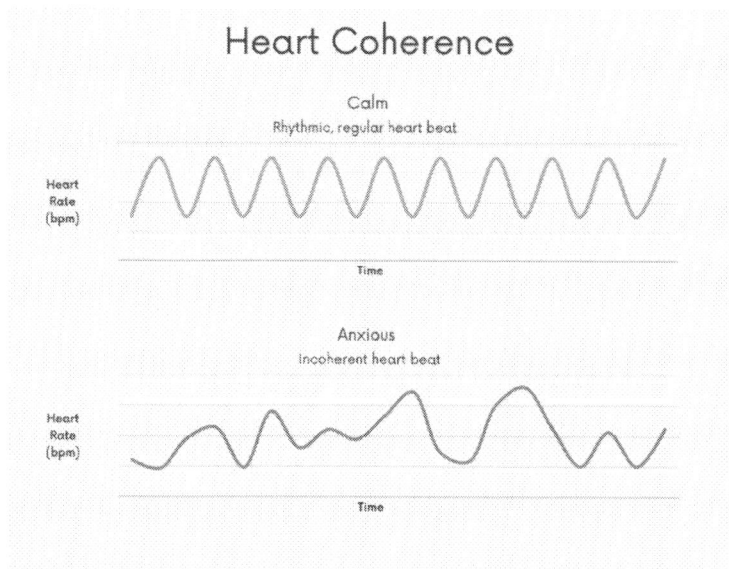

Heart Coherence

Calm
Rhythmic, regular heart beat

Heart Rate (bpm)

Time

Anxious
Incoherent heart beat

Heart Rate (bpm)

Time

It's easy to start practicing cardiac coherence. The basic technique is breathing in for five seconds and breathing out for five seconds. You do this for "365," which stands for <u>three</u> times per day, <u>six</u> breaths per minute, for <u>five</u> minutes.[20]

Guided Relaxation

You can simply sit back or lie down and listen to the ten-minute guided relaxation available at facingyouranxiety.com. It's

---

[20] David O'Hare, *Heart Coherence 365: A Guide to Long Lasting Heart Coherence* (France: Thierry Souccar Editions, 2014).

designed to gently invite your mind and body to release tension and relax.

Rest and Relax. Do Something Fun.

Another way to activate the parasympathetic nervous system is to simply rest and relax. Before you start booing me off the stage for stating the obvious, please hear me out. We really do have to rest, relax, and have fun each and every day. It's underrated. I didn't realize this all my life until I met my husband, the king of fun, who seemed to make it a priority to relax every day doing something he enjoys. At first, it puzzled me why he would prioritize something so "unproductive" as having fun, but I saw that when he had his daily dose of relaxation, he was in a better mood, more present, and healthier. And the opposite was true when he didn't.

If you are prone to chronic anxiety, chances are you may also struggle with allowing yourself to have fun without feeling guilty or pressured to be productive. Having fun doesn't mean going out and partying every day. It means doing something *you* enjoy, just because it makes you feel good, and doing it guilt-free. For some people, it might be walking in nature. For others, it could be playing sports and doing an intense physical activity. It can be reading a fun novel, taking a hot shower or bath, playing games, making candles, playing with dogs, deal hunting, joking around with friends, or cooking. Whatever yours might be, doing something fun that grabs your attention and makes you happy is a good way to counteract fight-or-flight and bring yourself into a more balanced way of being. It's not just self-care. In our world, where we are constantly bombarded with messages of threat, having fun every day is a must, so I suggest you start taking it seriously!

10

Interrupting the Patterns

Have you ever decided to change unhealthy habits, only to see yourself returning to the same old habits after a short while? Consider the following stories.

[1]

This is the third time he's done this. What's wrong with him? Or is it me? Why do I always end up with jerks? Lauren gets up and down from her couch, feeling restless and awful. She walks over to her kitchen and reaches for the box of cookies. It occurs to her that she is on day eight of her diet. But it all feels pointless to her. All she wants to do right now is to eat and forget. She brings the cookies back to her couch and turns on the TV as she makes a mental note to place an order for pizza in half an hour and order some dessert. She knows she's going to regret it, but it doesn't matter right now.

[2]

Matt woke up with a sore throat, swollen eyelids, and a headache. Panic starts to set in. *What can this be? I'm feeling sick to my stomach. Are my eyes infected? What if I go blind?* Having struggled with health anxiety for years, he knows what will happen next. He'll spend the whole day googling his symptoms, thinking of worst-case scenarios, and calling his doctor for the earliest possible appointment. He won't be able to do anything else but obsess over the slightest changes in his symptoms. Logically, Matt knows it's likely a common cold, but he also knows that's not going to change how his day is going to unfold.

[3]

Tossing and turning, Jen is unable to fall asleep. She feels anxious and upset and can't stop thinking about the argument with her partner, Tom. *This is all his fault. I didn't deserve that kind of treatment. He needs to know.* Jen gets up from the couch and marches into their bedroom, where Tom is trying to sleep. A part of her knows that the argument this late at night will only escalate things between them. It's happened countless times. It's as if she can see the doomed future, which looks almost the same as the past, where they yell and swear, throw character accusations, and threaten to end the relationship. But in this moment, it doesn't matter to Jen. She needs to let him have it. Right now.

Look for what these stories have in common. You can see that Lauren, Matt, and Jen knew what they were doing would harm them, but they did it anyway, as if a train following the tracks laid out ahead. I wonder if you can think of the times you became a passenger in your own life, engaging in the same old harmful patterns such as procrastination, worrying, obsessing, exploding in anger, and addictive behaviors, as if on autopilot. Once we return to our normal selves, we beat ourselves up and vow not to do it again. But those vows are often short-lived, and we find ourselves falling back into the old familiar patterns. Frustrating, isn't it?

I want to tell you that it's not your fault, and you can stop blaming yourself for failing to change. The truth is our brains are not designed to be conducive to change. Our brains have to be efficient to help with our survival and everyday functioning. Do you remember when it used to be hard to recite the multiplication table? What's 3 x 9? I'm guessing the answer almost immediately popped into your head. How useful. The efficiency of our brain is marvelous. Now try to forget what 3 x 9 is. You can't. You've already learned the answer and repeated it thousands of times in your head throughout your life. The neural pathways in your brain won't let you forget just because you want to. If you want to object and say this is an issue of memory, let's consider a different example. How about driving? When you are on the road, you can easily adjust your speed and react to the evolving situations around you, even if you were deep in thought about something that happened earlier and not thinking about driving at all. Is it possible to try and force yourself to consciously think about when exactly to accelerate or brake? No, that would make driving quite dangerous as it would slow down your reaction time. Thankfully, your brain is efficient. It knows exactly what to do to keep you safe and avoid dangers on the road, and the execution (with your body) is almost automatic and effortless.

If our brains weren't efficient like this, how else would we have learned to speak languages, know and follow social cues (if someone says hi, you greet back), and perform daily tasks like brushing your teeth and showering? Imagine having to concentrate on exactly what we are doing every time we perform a simple act. It would be exhausting, and we probably wouldn't get much done throughout the day because everything would take a long time. With this knowledge, you can stop blaming yourself and learn to work with your brain to help you change. There are better ways to go about changing our harmful old patterns than to rely on willpower, logic, or morality (i.e., what's right or wrong).

To change unhealthy patterns, we need to understand what makes us continue to do what we do, even when we know it's not good for us. Here's what each of our patterns looks like when broken down. First, there is a trigger. For Matt, it was waking up with symptoms of illness. The trigger evokes certain emotions: fear, anxiety, and panic in Matt's case. These emotions guide our way into unhelpful but familiar (and therefore easy and comfortable from the brain's perspective) behaviors, which, for Matt, are worrying and catastrophizing. These behaviors, of course, lead to an undesirable outcome as Matt ended up having a miserable, unproductive day. It's like a chain reaction starting with a trigger and ending with an undesirable outcome.

The Chain Reaction

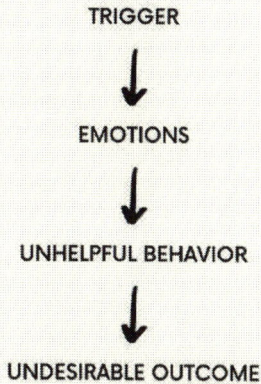

TRIGGER

↓

EMOTIONS

↓

UNHELPFUL BEHAVIOR

↓

UNDESIRABLE OUTCOME

Matt's Health Anxiety

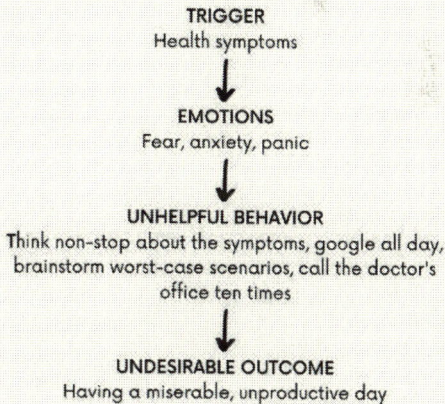

TRIGGER
Health symptoms

↓

EMOTIONS
Fear, anxiety, panic

↓

UNHELPFUL BEHAVIOR
Think non-stop about the symptoms, google all day,
brainstorm worst-case scenarios, call the doctor's
office ten times

↓

UNDESIRABLE OUTCOME
Having a miserable, unproductive day

Here are two more patterns that people often struggle with:

Example: Procrastination

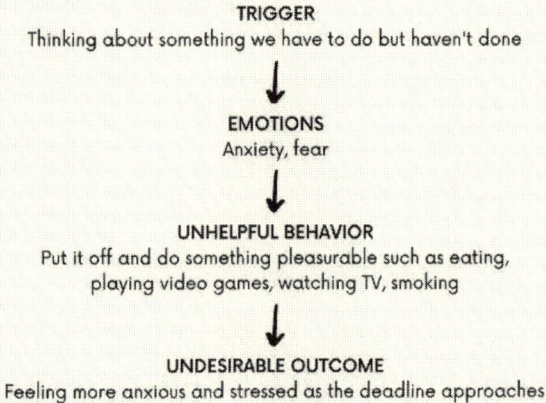

TRIGGER
Thinking about something we have to do but haven't done

↓

EMOTIONS
Anxiety, fear

↓

UNHELPFUL BEHAVIOR
Put it off and do something pleasurable such as eating,
playing video games, watching TV, smoking

↓

UNDESIRABLE OUTCOME
Feeling more anxious and stressed as the deadline approaches

Example: Self-Criticism

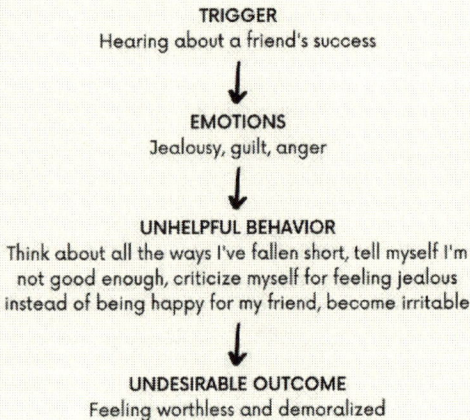

TRIGGER
Hearing about a friend's success

↓

EMOTIONS
Jealousy, guilt, anger

↓

UNHELPFUL BEHAVIOR
Think about all the ways I've fallen short, tell myself I'm
not good enough, criticize myself for feeling jealous
instead of being happy for my friend, become irritable

↓

UNDESIRABLE OUTCOME
Feeling worthless and demoralized

Consider pausing here to think about and write out your own patterns. What are some patterns that aren't serving you that you'd like to change? It might help to go back to Chapter 5, Facing Your Anxiety, to review your answers.

With the help of the techniques in this chapter, we can interrupt and break these patterns. It's easier than you think. We only need to introduce one more step to break the chain reaction from a trigger to an undesirable outcome. The additional step is where you perform a pattern interrupt technique.

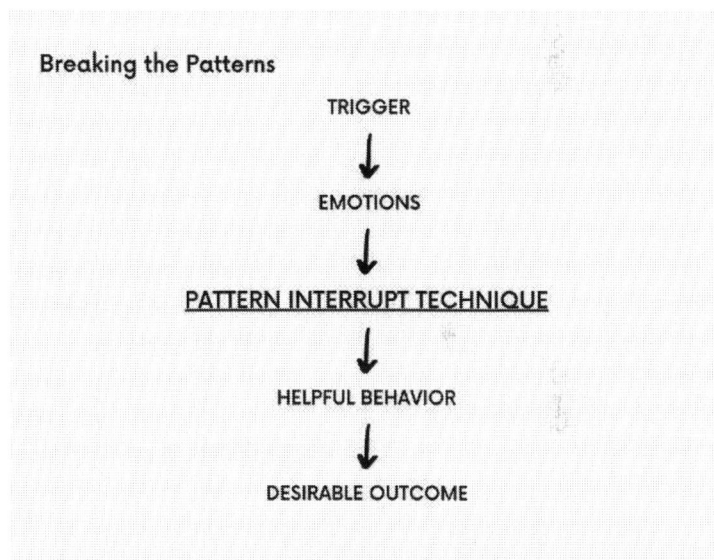

Breaking the Patterns

TRIGGER

↓

EMOTIONS

↓

<u>PATTERN INTERRUPT TECHNIQUE</u>

↓

HELPFUL BEHAVIOR

↓

DESIRABLE OUTCOME

When you read about other people's patterns above and consider your own patterns, you'll realize that it's the strong emotions that compel us towards the same behaviors, which are unhelpful but make sense in our minds. Your unconscious mind performs a very simple act of reasoning: *I feel terrible. Eating/drinking/ smoking makes me feel good, so I'll do that now. I feel anxious, so I'll just keep worrying and thinking and see if I can solve these problems in my head. I feel angry, so I'm going to yell at the person who caused it.* These actions are meant to provide us relief from painful emotions, but the relief given is temporary at best. And we all know what it's like to suffer the consequences of how we acted when emotions were running high.

To stop unhelpful behaviors and maybe even introduce helpful behaviors that lead to desirable outcomes, we need to take care of our emotions first. The pain of guilt, shame, and anger can be hard to cope with. But what if you knew exactly what to do with them without turning to the same old behaviors for relief?

The two techniques I'm about to share with you are designed to take the edge off any intense painful emotions and restore inner balance. Imagine what it would be like to no longer be swept off your feet at the whim of your triggers and out-of-control emotions. Knowing how to return to a more grounded place from an emotional turmoil frees us up to consciously *choose* our responses instead of mindlessly following what feels familiar. We can choose thoughts and actions that serve us well and are good and healthy for us, reclaiming the power to live our lives how we want to.

Before I learned that I could relieve emotional pain on my own, I lived in fear of emotions. My thoughts and actions, at the core, had only one objective: preventing and avoiding all past, present, and future pains. I was always worried about something, such as people close to me dying or leaving me, being broke, and embarrassing myself. I was also often paralyzed with indecision. *If I do this, will this go out of control and make me anxious? If I don't, will I feel guilty and awful? Which would be worse? What if I can't cope?* To be fair, I had good reasons to make it my primary objective to avoid pain, having gone through episodes of clinical depression so painful that it nearly took my life. I never wanted to return to that place again if I could help it. I feared anxiety and its cascading effects that could easily lead to depression. Trauma, unfortunately, teaches us to fear and avoid its repetition at all costs. Thus, I lived in a prison of my own fears, making decisions that kept me safe, albeit somewhat unhappy and dissatisfied with my life.

Although my journey had taught me to accept myself, practice self-compassion, and do everything else I've shown you so far in this book, I could not shake off the lingering fear of pain. But thankfully, at this point in my journey, I was at least open-minded and willing to try things that intellectually didn't make sense. That is when I started coming across these pattern interrupt techniques. If practicing breathing techniques and relaxation was like taking vitamins, using these techniques was like applying first aid and taking painkillers. The more I used the techniques to soothe emotional pain on my own in desperate moments, the more I felt in control. It eventually started to click that emotions are not to be feared. Yes, they hurt, but I can deal with them as they come up. From that point, I, not the fear of emotions, became the captain of my own ship, free to take my life where I wanted. I was no longer preoccupied with avoiding pain and obstacles and kept my eye on the destination where there is joy and meaning.

Do you also struggle with fear of emotional pain? Is this fear keeping you stuck in unhealthy patterns and decisions that limit your potential? It's time to start learning that you are and have always been in charge of your emotions. Emotions are there to provide you with helpful information and serve you, not the other way around. Learn and start using the following techniques to put emotions in their rightful place and reclaim the power to choose your thoughts and actions.

Emotional Freedom Technique (EFT Tapping)

The Emotional Freedom Technique (EFT) is one of the most powerful therapeutic techniques I often share with my clients. As a skeptic, it took me some time to test it and determine that it actually works. In fact, it worked the first time I used it, which left me puzzled because it didn't make logical sense. But firsthand experience and evidence speak volumes. Not only did I receive positive results and feedback from countless clients, but more than 100 research studies demonstrate EFT's efficacy. For a bibliography of EFT research, you can visit EFT Universe (https://eftuniverse.com/research-studies/).

Here is how you perform this technique. You can refer to the chart below for the tapping points.

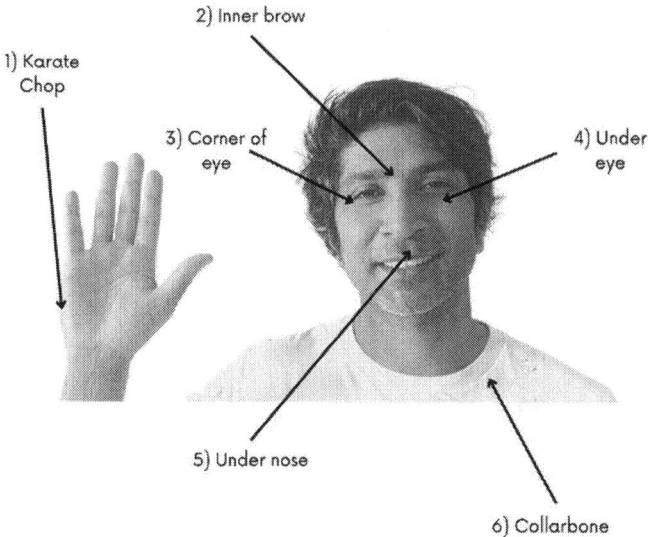

When you are triggered, or there is something that troubles you emotionally, label it (e.g., anxiety, anger) and rate the intensity from 0 to 10.

1. Start tapping on the karate chop point on either hand with three fingers saying this setup phrase silently to yourself or out loud: "Even though I have this anxiety [guilt, shame, fear, etc.], I completely love and accept myself. I'm choosing to let this go."

2. Next, tap on the inner brow (either side), saying, "It's OK to let this go." Tap at least seven times (it doesn't have to be exact) before moving on to the next tapping point.

3. Now, tap on the outside corner of your eyes (either side with one hand or both sides with two hands; the same applies to #4), saying, "It's safe to let this go."

4. Tap under the eyes on your eye sockets, saying, "Let it go."

5. Then, tap under your nose above your lips, saying, "Let it go."

6. Lastly, tap on your collarbone either with one or two hands, saying, "Let it go."

7. Take a slow, big breath in, and breathe out evenly and slowly.

8. Check in with yourself and rate the intensity from 0 to 10. You'll notice that it has decreased. Repeat the cycle one or more times if it's not at or close to 0.

Expanding Awareness Technique

Emotional Freedom Tapping is great, but it doesn't hurt to learn more than one technique to work with difficult emotions so you have options. You can use this technique, Expanding Awareness, anytime and anywhere you want, and even when you are in public, no one will know you are doing anything. It has a grounding effect and can restore your perspective when emotions start to hijack your mind. It's also a fun exercise that activates your sense of imagination and creativity.

1. First, sit comfortably (but you can do it in any position once you've learned how to do it).

2. Pick a spot in front of you and stare at it for a moment. It's best to pick a spot at least three feet away.

3. Relax your eyes and expand your peripheral vision all the way both to your right and left. Now, imagine your vision continues to expand endlessly, and you can see through the walls going beyond the physical space you are in.

4. Imagine the expanded vision is 360 degrees now and you can see through the walls in front of you and also behind your back as if you have an X-ray vision in full colors. You can also see beyond the sky into the universe and below the ground all the way to the core of the earth.

5. Enjoy the sensation of being able to see all things at the same time.

6. When you are ready, slowly return to the present awareness, starting to notice the physical objects you are seeing and reorienting yourself back into the space you are in.

The best way to learn these techniques is to simply use them repeatedly in response to anxiety and other difficult emotions. Now that you have them in your emotional first aid kit, you can feel free to use either or both anytime you think will be helpful. And don't worry if these techniques don't completely remove the uncomfortable emotions. They are not meant to solve our emotional problems. I recommend you use them to interrupt any unhealthy patterns you've identified for yourself and to break the chain reaction of emotions leading to unhealthy behaviors and coping. Then, you can make conscious choices from a grounded place that pave the way to healthy behaviors and desirable outcomes in various areas of your life, making your way towards freedom from anxiety.

11

Empowering Through Self-Hypnosis

I think I can. I think I can. I think I can.

– Watty Piper, *The Little Engine That Could*

How much do you believe in yourself? What's your sense of self-belief when you face a task or goal, whether big or small, that you want to accomplish? Do you often feel unsure if you can or think you can't?

Anxiety erodes self-confidence. It's a small voice in your head that keeps asking the same question: can I handle it? Sometimes the voice grows stronger and stronger until it takes over entirely, and it becomes a fact: "No, I can't handle it." That's what happened following my initial anxiety attack. It started with doubts. The things I used to accomplish with ease somehow became questionable. When I wrote emails, the voice intruded: *Are you sure you phrased it the right way? Maybe you don't know what you are talking about.* In social situations, it monitored my speech with vigilance: *You said it wrong. Now they think you are dumb. You should've prepared better.* It even came in when I played soccer, my favorite sport, judging and second-guessing every move I made during the game: *You are not ready for this. You are just going to embarrass yourself.* It slowed down my reaction time and sucked the joy out of it. I grew increasingly timid, reserved, and reluctant in all areas of life. The constant self-doubt became so painful that I started to just say no to responsibilities and opportunities. I stepped down from all leadership positions I held. It all felt like too much. That, of course, further damaged my self-confidence. Once a confident self-proclaimed trailblazer, I no longer believed I was capable of achieving much in life.

Many people seek help for anxiety in a similar state of disempowerment. Failures and anxiety go hand in hand. Then, we start feeling like we are a failure. We won't amount to much, so we may as well seek safety and security. We start limiting ourselves. That dream job that we once wanted? It's going to be too much. I don't think I can be a good leader. I won't be able to handle all that stress and responsibility. The ideal romantic relationship we once pursued? Well, relationships are too hard. It didn't work out last time. I was miserable and felt stuck. The breakup was awful. Why bother? We learn to settle. I'll never be able to afford a house like that. We get good at surviving and curtailing expectations. We become risk averse, expecting and trying to prevent the downside rather than getting excited about the upside and the potential gains. Chronic anxiety is exhausting and eventually drives us to want to play things safe, if not to the extent I describe, in more subtle ways such as keeping our mouths shut during meetings, avoiding intimacy in relationships, and not actively seeking new challenges that can bring fulfillment and growth.

Look inside yourself and consider whether you may have been limiting yourself, citing anxiety as the cause. Have you been afraid of changes? Do you struggle to think about or say what you want for fear that you may fail and not get it? If the answer is no, that's great news. But if a part of you feels beaten down by anxiety into submission, I've been there too. And I'm here to tell you there is a way to reclaim power and build unyielding self-confidence.

Monica sought therapy after suffering multiple anxiety attacks that began interfering with her corporate executive career. Having experienced continuous successes in her life and career, she wasn't used to feeling insecure and doubting her abilities. When she finally decided to get help, she was on stress leave from work and had stopped most of the activities she used to enjoy, such as playing competitive sports, baking, and traveling. She thought mental health was for the "weak" and she didn't need to be "fixed." She was a high-functioning person and had been able to push through uncomfortable feelings for most of her life up until now when things took a turn for the worse.

Through gentle exploration and reframing, Monica began to understand the power of her mind, that she didn't need to be fixed, but that didn't mean she couldn't get an upgrade. She learned about how her own mind creates anxiety and the alternative ways to use her mind so that she can create positive states of mind and achieve desired outcomes. Thus far, she had coped with the pressure to perform by overpreparing and being ready as much as possible for all things that could go wrong. While she had been successful, that kind of functioning was taking a toll on her body and mind, which she realized was a big reason for reaching a breaking point.

Monica decided to let go of using brute effort and start doing things differently. She now understood that she had used fear of failure to motivate herself and push harder but that it eventually backfired, crippling her with severe anxiety. She was determined to reprogram her mind and let go of her fears, and her technique of choice was self-hypnosis. During self-hypnosis, she could have positive experiences and feel in control ahead of the events she had become so used to dreading and expecting the worst. It was eye-opening for her to know that she could shape future events in her head and make them happen in real life, of course, with some focused time and effort. This way felt much easier and certainly more fun than expecting the worst and preparing for unfavorable consequences. Gradually, her attitude and expectancy shifted for the better, restoring her optimism, zest for life, and confidence. She also became more in tune with her needs and wants now that she knew she didn't have to hold herself back all the time. She now teaches yoga in her spare time while contemplating transitioning out of her corporate career eventually to teach full-time. In the meantime, Monica feels like a new person and finds more ease each day since returning to work.

Would you like to learn a powerful skill to overcome your fears and take charge of your life, as Monica did? Read on, and I'll show you when and how to use self-hypnosis.

Setting Anxiety Aside

Before we get to how to perform self-hypnosis, I want to explain how this approach is unique and different from all the previous techniques you've learned. Using self-hypnosis is a proactive strategy. If thus far, you've been conditioned to *respond* to anxiety when it inevitably arises, this strategy will change your perspective. When you are proactive, you are no longer on the defensive. You don't try to prevent anxiety or even let go of it when it happens. Your objective is something entirely different because self-hypnosis aims to *create* what you want in your life. Do you want more anxiety in your life? Probably not, so you start thinking and imagining something you want, like feeling calm and confident, performing at your best, having a dream vacation, and so on. In effect, you are making anxiety *irrelevant*.

To be clear, you are not ignoring anxiety or pretending it doesn't exist. You are just turning your attention to something else for the time being because we can only truly focus on one thing at a time (in case you are wondering, multitasking isn't real; we simply switch attention from one thing to another really quickly to the point it feels like we are doing them all at the same time). Also, if you are feeling awesome and like on top of the world on a regular basis, does anxiety even matter? At its best, anxiety will be fleeting and pass quickly. Thus, it becomes irrelevant. It no longer undermines your quality of life.

When to Use Self-Hypnosis

You can use self-hypnosis for many purposes. Here are some examples:

To change how you think and feel about situations and activities that tend to make you anxious
- Presentations
- Fear of flying
- Social gatherings
- Dating and sexual problems

To improve your performance in pretty much anything
- Sports
- Job interviews
- Competitions

To change unwanted habits
- Substance use
- Diet
- Obsessive/addictive behaviors

To improve health and recover from injuries and pain

- Physical fitness
- Pregnancy and childbirth
- Chronic pain
- Irritable bowel syndrome

To unwind and relax

What is Self-Hypnosis?

To understand self-hypnosis, let's first consider hypnosis. Hypnosis is a state of focus and absorption. It's an altered state of consciousness that's different from the waking, analytical consciousness we are usually in.

We naturally experience this state in and out throughout the day, so it's not necessarily a mysterious state that the media often makes it out to be. For example, when watching a good movie or TV show, we get sucked into the story and forget the time. Have you ever had a "driving trance" where you arrived at your destination but didn't remember how you got there because your mind was somewhere else? Daydreaming is also an example of a trance state (a state of hypnosis).

When we are in hypnosis, our critical, analytical minds calm down, and we become more open to new ways of seeing things. This is a good place to be when trying to make personal changes to live a better life. In this state, we no longer have to repeat the same thoughts, feelings, and actions that keep us stuck in our old familiar patterns. Instead, we become the creator of our own future. I mentioned in Chapter 2 that we have an unconscious mind, a storehouse of everything we've ever experienced and a gatekeeper that protects us from harm. Hypnosis opens a channel to our unconscious mind so we can work directly with it for healing and growth.

Self-hypnosis is a practice of entering this state, let's call it trance, on your own, anytime and anywhere you wish.

Practicing Easy Self-Hypnosis

Self-Hypnosis Induction

In hypnosis, the process of entering trance is called induction, and the hypnotist gives instructions or uses a set of words and phrases (suggestions) to help induce trance. And in self-hypnosis, you'll be giving yourself instructions and suggestions to help yourself enter a trance. Entering this state is a prerequisite for using one of the self-hypnosis techniques I'll show you in this chapter.

First, let me describe what you are aiming for: what trance feels like and how you'll know you are ready to move on to the techniques. The media often misrepresents hypnosis. In a recent movie, a hypnotist is seen telling her subject to go to the "sunken place," and the subject falls unconscious. I want to emphasize that trance doesn't mean unconscious. Especially in the context of self-hypnosis, we are merely looking to get into a state of relaxed focus, like when you are watching a movie or reading a book that absorbs your attention. It's called light trance. You can feel free to go into a deeper level of trance, but you don't have to.

With practice, it becomes easier and easier to go into trance. There are many ways to achieve this state, so once you've learned the techniques I'll introduce, you can feel free to experiment and tailor a method that works best for you. You can add, remove, or tweak the steps I describe here.

Step 1: Keeping your head straight, roll your eyes up towards the ceiling. Hold this position for a few seconds, take a deep breath in, and as you exhale, close your eyes and let them relax.

Step 2: Take a moment to relax each part of your body—facial muscles, jaws, neck and shoulders, arms, hands, back, stomach, buttocks, thighs, calves, and feet. You can simply place your attention on one part of your body at a time and relax, releasing any tension.

Step 3: Count down from 10 to 1, telling yourself you are going deeper and more relaxed. For example:

10 . . . going deeper

9 . . . going deeper

8 . . . more relaxed

7 . . . deeper and deeper

And so on (you can simply repeat the same phrase "going deeper" or "deeper and deeper").

<u>Step 4</u>: Use the self-hypnosis techniques (described below).

<u>Step 5</u>: To come out of hypnosis, start turning your attention to your breath, back to the present, wiggling your fingers and moving your body a little, and open your eyes when ready.

While relaxation is not hypnosis, it's an effective gateway to trance. To assist with relaxation, you can utilize slow deep breathing, making your in-breath and out-breath longer to activate the parasympathetic nervous system.

With practice, you'll experience that on some days, you can easily go into trance, sometimes by just closing your eyes and taking a few seconds to relax, while on other days, you may need some time to go through each of the steps described above. There is no right or wrong way to do this. Learn to listen to your body and mind and follow your intuition.

Techniques of Self-Hypnosis

#1: Autosuggestions/Affirmations

I used to hate affirmations. They seemed too easy and oversimplified, which annoyed me.

Me: *I don't feel good about myself.*

Self-Help Book: *Tell yourself you are worthy and you deserve love! Repeat after me: I'm worthy. I'm lovable.*

I tried half-heartedly, and it didn't work. Well, I'm recommending it now, so you might wonder what has changed and what is different about the method I'm about to tell you. What I learned about affirmations since then is that it's all about the feelings. To experience the full benefit of an affirmation, when you tell yourself the affirmation, for the time being, you need to suspend your doubts, believe it, and feel what follows from it if it were true.

If this is a bit confusing, think about what happens when you tell yourself something like, "I'm no good. I don't think I can do this." Doesn't it feel true and you feel the emotions from it, such as sad, disheartened, hopeless, and agitated? Yet, it's just a statement, not an absolute truth such as "the sun rises every morning." Whether we realize it or not, we often tell ourselves negative affirmations to great effect because we believe and feel them.

Now, I'm asking you to do the opposite. You'll tell yourself a positive affirmation, believe it, and feel the emotions that naturally flow from it. In case you are protesting, "But I really don't buy it," let me remind you that you are on a path to making anxiety irrelevant, which requires changing how you think and feel, especially about yourself. Do you want to change? If you do, then it's time to get some new beliefs. When I was depressed and anxious, I believed "the world is a dangerous place and people are going to hurt me." The statement felt true to the core. But as long as I believed it to be true, I wasn't going to get better. I needed to get to "the world provides unlimited potential, and it's safe, fun, and good for me to be alive." It was quite the leap, so I took baby steps to try on the new belief one moment at a time, experiencing it just for the time being until it permeated my mind and life. By practicing this, we are also making new neural connections and strengthening them the more we practice it, which makes it easier the next time we do it. If we keep at it, sooner or later it will become an unconscious habit and we'll be living out the new belief without even realizing it.

So here is how you can practice affirmations in self-hypnosis. Choose an affirmation or a few that you'd like to practice. I'll give you an example. Affirmations can also be called autosuggestions (suggestions you give yourself). Émile Coué was a psychologist and pharmacist who pioneered autosuggestions. He taught his patients to say to themselves, "Every day, in every way, I am getting better and better," which resulted in actual healing and improvements in their medical conditions. Try saying it to yourself a few times:

Every day, in every way, I am getting better and better.

Every day, in every way, I am getting better and better.

Every day, in every way, I am getting better and better.

If you are apprehensive about affirmations, I suggest you start with the Émile Coué affirmation which is simple, nonthreatening, and highly effective. While you can practice affirmations anytime without the self-hypnosis induction, I've found that going first into a state of relaxed focus makes it even better and more effective.

Here are some affirmations you might like:

- I am in charge of my own life.
- I matter. My voice matters.
- I am strong.
- I choose to forgive. I forgive.
- I choose to feel joy (peace, calm, etc.).
- I am worthy.
- I am loved.
- It's safe for me to be happy.

You can also write your own affirmations that are meaningful for you, such as "Life is happening for me" and "God loves me." Whatever you wish to choose, make sure you say it in the *present tense* (rather than past or future), and it's *positive*. You don't want to say, "I am not anxious, I am not insecure," because saying the words anxious and insecure tend to trigger the feelings associated with them. Instead, you can say, "I am calm. I am safe and secure."

#2: Visualization

Visualization is a true workhorse of self-hypnosis. If you learn to visualize, you can make all kinds of positive changes. The only limit is your imagination. Remember how imagined events and actual events are kind of the same from our brains' perspective? You will use this knowledge to your full advantage by imagining your heart's desires as if they are happening right now. This is basically how hypnosis helps people change. Applying this method, my clients have achieved remarkable results starting from external changes such as quitting cigarettes and alcohol, losing weight through healthy diet and exercise, and getting promotions and new jobs, to internal changes such as staying in good mental and physical health during times of stress, healing from past trauma, being more self-compassionate and loving.

If you tend to find it hard to visualize, don't worry. The process I describe here makes it easier for you to start visualizing. Even if you still find it hard to "see" any images in your mind's eye, that doesn't mean you have to give up on this technique. You'll still benefit from thinking about or holding the ideas (of what you intend to visualize) in your mind.

An easy way to learn visualization is to recreate a pleasurable event you've already experienced. Here is how. Following self-hypnosis induction, bring to mind the event you want to experience again. For example, it could be a time you spent hiking in the mountains. Now, choose a specific scene from the hike. Maybe it was when you were at the top of the mountain, looking around and taking in the beautiful panoramic view of the valley.

See it in the first person, i.e., through your own eyes (not in the third person, where you see your own body).

Notice what you see. Notice the colors you see in your mind's eye. Make them vivid.

Notice what you hear, the wind and the rustling of the trees.

Notice what you smell. Perhaps you can smell the scent of the pine trees.

Notice how your body feels in the moment. Maybe the sensations of stepping on rocks and touching a tree.

Notice any emotions and feelings you have in that place: serene, hopeful, and a sense of accomplishment.

Now it's your turn. Close your eyes and re-experience a pleasurable event from the past. You can do this with or without the self-hypnosis induction. Use this quick summary to fully recreate the experience in your mind:

See (colors), hear, smell, notice body sensations, and feel.

How did you like it? Are you surprised to find how easily you can bring back positive experiences from the past? Here is food for thought. As with affirmations, we can easily relive negative events on repeat without even realizing it. Following a fight with our spouse or friend, we might think about (which is basically visualizing) all the ways they mistreated us in the past. We may also visualize all the pain from a divorce or fallout from the relationship. And, of course, when we do this, our mind and body experience this as if it's real and bring back the negative effect from this visualization. Think about how you may have self-hypnotized yourself to re-experience negative events on repeat. Turn things around by practicing visualization for what you want and what's good and healthy for yourself instead.

Now that you've practiced visualization using past events, you can start visualizing anything you want using the same principles. Choose what you want to create. Say you have a tennis match coming up. Go to the scene, at the start of the match, in your mind. See and take in the atmosphere. Feel the racket in your hand and give it a few swings. You are feeling confident, ready, and calm. You are hitting the ball exactly how you intend and see the ball precisely hitting the spot in the court you were aiming for. You feel fully in control of your body and mind. You hear the audience cheering and feel the excitement.

Julie used visualization to change her beliefs about family gatherings which she dreaded due to the judgmental attitude of some family members. In her visualization, she experienced feeling grounded and confident and standing up for herself and her cousins when her aunts started being inappropriately critical. She also experienced a sense of detachment from the criticism and saw her aunts' behaviors from a higher perspective, noticing how insecure they looked. The next time she went to a family dinner, she could relax and enjoy her time there rather than be vigilant.

What positive changes would you like to create with the power of self-hypnosis?

12

Transcending Anxiety

You were born with wings, why prefer to crawl through life?

— Rumi

To free ourselves from the suffering of anxiety, we need to transcend it. We need to become greater than anxiety. The knowledge, tools, and techniques you've learned so far equip you to handle daily struggles skillfully. But there is more. At the beginning, we established that we need to keep our eyes on the forest, not the trees. Transcending anxiety is not about knowing exactly what to do when something happens. By doing that, you are still on the same level as anxiety, which means you are merely good at responding correctly and minimizing the damage. What if you don't have to stop there? What if you can use this chapter of your life (no pun intended) to elevate yourself to the point that the problems in your life, anxiety included, don't really matter anymore? To be clear, I'm not saying you stop caring about them. You'll still care about what goes on in your life, but you'll have a sense of knowing: "I can deal with whatever may happen. I am safe." When you have this knowledge, that's when anxiety becomes insignificant and a passing feeling.

I told you in Chapter 1 that anxiety is like an annoying friend that showed up in your life to guide you to a better life. When you understand and start to treat yourself with kindness and acceptance, something changes inside. You don't tear yourself apart whenever you fall short of your expectations. Instead, you tend to your wounds, encourage yourself, and ask, "What can I learn from this?" You start developing the courage to challenge yourself because failure doesn't cause unbearable pain and shame. When you dedicate your time and effort to helping yourself with the tools and techniques, you'll experience positive results and changes. This empowers you, and you may start to wonder what else you are capable of achieving. You start to develop a sense of trust. Life becomes more enjoyable and exciting when you are in the driver's seat. You may become aware of some ways you've been limiting yourself and allow yourself to be honest with your desires and passions. It becomes safe to be authentic, to be you.

My journey with anxiety paved the way to authenticity and freedom. I no longer feel ashamed of who I am. Fear of failure doesn't stop me from doing what my heart desires, such as writing this book and sharing my personal experience with you. It's actually fun talking about my failures and struggles because I know I'm greater than those, and we can all learn from my shortcomings. They don't define me in any sense. When I feel the pain of guilt, shame, anger, fear, and anxiety, I can let them go and return to a place of peace and trust. Life is full of possibilities, and most of the time, I'm excited and eager to see what's ahead. Or better yet, what I can learn and create in my life.

I've come a long way since the breakdown on the subway. It all started with getting to know who I am, especially my fears and struggles. At times, I fell into the trap of endlessly analyzing my flaws and how I was going to fix them. But I started to see that I'm a person, not a tool, just like everyone I love. A person has worth and dignity. I connected with others who were also going through a hard time and practiced empathy for myself just as I had empathy for them. I became increasingly aware of the inner self-critical voice and stopped siding with it. It felt awkward, but I practiced being my own advocate as much as possible. Gradually, the critical voice subsided because I wasn't really interested in it anymore. It was like letting go of an unhealthy friendship. When you stop contacting and hanging out with them, they gradually disappear from your life. More than anything, practicing self-compassion helped me heal from past trauma. I can't change what happened in the past, but I can always treat myself better today. When there is an inner advocate who is always there for you, it gets easier to forgive yourself and others and let go of past grievances.

Mindfulness played a big role in noticing when I was triggered, anxious, and self-critical. Without mindfulness, I would've fallen into the trap of being sucked into the familiar unhelpful coping strategies like drinking, obsessing, and exhausting my body by overworking and overexercising. It was tough, and I certainly failed from time to time. But I held on to the intention that I would change and heal from anxiety and depression. During this time, I let go of the guilt that I wasn't sitting down to meditate for long periods. I knew I was getting better through short but regular practices.

Catching myself when I was avoiding, worrying, what-if-ing, and catastrophizing became fun because I never realized until I started to pay attention how much these habits occupied my mind. The biggest one for me was what-if-ing. I noticed that whenever I felt anxious, I was imagining things that could go wrong, i.e., what-if-ing, which led to other unhelpful behaviors like analysis paralysis, overworking, and procrastinating. When I caught myself what-if-ing, I laughed inside a little and intentionally imagined a great scenario I would love to have happen. It was interesting to me how, with a bit of mindfulness and intention, I could be more glass half-full than half-empty at will. It was freeing to detach from my thoughts and direct them where I wanted them to go. I developed a better outlook on life and became more optimistic and grateful.

I started to treat my body better as well. I learned the difference between tension and relaxation. As my body had been starved for relaxation, the effect of deep breathing made a big difference, and I tried to guide my body into that state of relaxation as often as I could. I noticed my mind was calm when my body was calm and vice versa. Things felt easier and better when my body was in a good place. I stopped drinking coffee every day and reduced my sugar intake, noticing that it was throwing my body off balance.

A breakthrough came when I started using pattern interrupt techniques whenever I was triggered. Before then, I had never felt truly confident about my ability to keep my emotions under control. I was scared of feeling scared, anxious, depressed, or ashamed because I thought I might fall into a deep hole I couldn't escape. But I was able to prove to myself over and over again that I was in charge of my feelings, thoughts, and behaviors. Being unafraid of negative emotions that could result from rejection and failures, I started to take more risks and do and ask for what I wanted. I could handle it. And using self-hypnosis allowed me to be creative and start dreaming again, as I used to when I was young. My only limits were the extent of my imagination. This book is the outcome of my imagination. Before I could write a book, I needed to believe that I was capable of writing a book, and I achieved this through self-hypnosis.

Greater Than My Problem

When Debbie first came to work with me, she thought I would help eradicate her anxiety. She suffered from irritable bowel syndrome and speech problems in public. She put in the work and did everything I asked of her, faithfully using the tools and techniques she learned and regularly reflecting on our discussions.

To her disappointment, her speech issues continued. One day, she felt exasperated and emotional during one of our sessions. She said, "this is not what I expected. I thought I would've gotten rid of this problem by now." A part of me was taken aback as my immediate thought was, *You should've resolved this issue for her by now*, but I quickly brought myself back and explored what was on her mind. Our discussions led to her realizing all the gains she wasn't seeing when she focused on the problem. She was treating herself with kindness and compassion. She was more comfortable with her emotions and able to express them as she did just now. This was something she had struggled with very much as she tended to ignore or repress them. She knew that difficult feelings pass and wasn't scared of them anymore. The things she used to be scared of, she even enjoyed from time to time, such as giving presentations and making small talk with colleagues. Once she connected the dots, the problem didn't seem like a problem anymore. While it was still there, she had outgrown her problem. The next time I saw her, she had an air of confidence about her. We talked about the problem briefly but quickly moved on to other important topics, such as how she's been growing as a person and what's next for her.

I Am More Than That

Liam used to be a star at his workplace. People looked up to him as a future leader of the company. Problems started when he started clashing with his new boss, who micromanaged and kept a tight leash on Liam, which he wasn't used to. At the end of the year, the boss gave him an average rating. To Liam, it was a serious blow. Never in his life was he called "average." Ambitious and driven by nature, he worked harder to meet expectations, putting in more hours and thinking about work every waking minute. It took a toll on his family. He was a father to a toddler, and his wife was going through depression. He sought help to remove anxiety so he could be more productive, think better, and achieve more in order to restore his reputation.

Liam was motivated to start learning the techniques to conquer his anxiety. He wasn't a stranger to self-development and had already tried many tactics to be more confident and well-presented. He reluctantly followed along when he was told that he needed to go deeper and get to know himself. When he got out of the analysis and fix-it mode and could simply be with his wounds from the past as a compassionate observer, tears flowed down, realizing he had never been gentle with himself. When he felt insecure, he pushed himself more and drove himself to the edge. It was usually sink or swim. He recalled how painful it was to grow up with a disability, feeling inferior to others and needing to always prove himself. That day, he promised himself to be his own advocate.

With his relationship with himself shifted, he noticed that he was becoming more resilient to judgment and criticism. It still hurt, but he could tend to the pain rather than react to it with unhelpful behaviors such as overcompensation by working harder (*I'll prove it to you*), self-criticism, and hypervigilance. His family life also improved as he became gentler and more compassionate with himself. He was able to be more vulnerable and patient with his wife and help out more at home.

From this place, he utilized the techniques of deep breathing, emotional freedom technique, and self-hypnosis to restore balance to his body and build confidence. Mindfulness was difficult for his busy mind, but he practiced for a short time here and there and intentionally directed his mind to the present a few times a day. He took better care of his body and respected his own limits, thinking, *It's possible to push through now, but I'm playing the long game and taking good care of myself.* It was difficult and anxiety-provoking to say no. At first, he was bombarded with thoughts like *What if they think I'm weak and incapable?* But he was able to use the tools and skills he learned to navigate the uncharted world of emotions to the best of his ability.

One day, while on a long walk by a lake, he felt an overwhelming sense of gratitude, despite the continuing difficulties at work and home. It just felt like everything was going to be okay. He looked back and appreciated how much he had changed. In that moment, he could care less if he was the star performer because he was way more and bigger than that. For the first time, he felt an inner sense of worth. The only person he needed validation from was himself.

The Power of Intention

"A journey of a thousand miles begins with a single step"
– Lao Tzu

Transcending anxiety is a life-changing journey. But without this single step, you'll have a hard time reaching your destination. The most important first step is this: setting a clear intention. This is a good time to revisit your intention. Why are you taking this journey? What's important for you?

Complete this sentence and remind yourself often why you are on this path to freedom from anxiety.

I intend to transcend my anxiety because

_____.

I am greater than anxiety.

By clarifying your intention, you are committing to seeing this journey through and receiving the fruits of your effort in due time. Sooner or later, you'll look back and realize how far you have come. When difficulties inevitably arise, return to your intention and switch to a higher perspective. Remind yourself that you are not trying to eliminate anxiety but to be higher and greater so that anxiety grows smaller and insignificant.

The Road to Transcendence

Now is your time. Here's a suggested process you can start right away and continue to practice that will pave your way to transcending anxiety:

Review the neuroscience of anxiety. The important principles to remember are the following:

- Anxiety is our body's response to perceived threats. Chronic anxiety is like a broken fire alarm going off when there's no threat.
- Feeling anxious is uncomfortable but not dangerous. However, there are long-term health consequences to chronic anxiety.
- Anxiety is learned and thus can be unlearned.
- Neurons that fire together wire together. The more you do something, the easier it becomes for you to do it. It cuts both ways. The more time you spend in anxiety, the easier it will be for you to feel anxious again. The more time you spend practicing the skills to tame your anxiety, the easier it will be for you to get out of the anxious state and also not fall into it (be triggered) in the first place.

Take time to get to know yourself and your anxiety. Be an observer. First, put on a scientist's hat to see what's going on. Then, become your own advocate. No one knows you better, so there's no one else better equipped to defend and care for you. It's okay to rely on loved ones occasionally, but do not delegate this responsibility to be your best friend and advocate.

Practice mini mindfulness exercises to strengthen your ability to become aware of, withstand waves of emotion, and create enough space to use the anxiety tools and techniques. While you don't have to sit down to meditate every day, remember to spend some time every day noticing the present moment while you are going about your day.

Be on the lookout for the four anxiety habits: (1) avoiding, (2) worrying, (3) what-if-ing, and (4) catastrophizing. Review Chapter 8 to know exactly what to do when you catch yourself engaging in one or more of these habits. The less time you spend with these unhelpful habits, the better and the faster you'll transcend your anxiety.

Practice deep breathing a few times daily to retrain your body and mind to spend more time in rest-and-digest rather than fight-or-flight. Enjoy the feelings of relaxation and learn to return to them at will. Intentionally engage in at least one fun and/or relaxing activity every day—something that makes you feel at ease. These practices and activities may not seem like much initially, but they add up and help you turn anxiety into a foreign state (i.e., not where you live) over time.

Take inventory of your unhealthy patterns and habits that have become automatic. They include your anxiety triggers. When you are triggered, pause to recognize and label emotions. Then, use pattern interrupt techniques (EFT tapping or expanding awareness) to self-soothe and break off the chain reaction that leads to undesirable behaviors and outcomes. Set an intention to stop letting emotions run your life and take charge of your emotions.

Lastly, use self-hypnosis to retrain yourself to think about what you want (e.g., calm, confident, happy) rather than what you don't want (e.g., not anxious, not insecure, not depressed). Using the self-hypnosis induction, practice positive affirmations and visualize your desires and dreams as if they are happening in real time. Make sure to suspend your doubts and feel the positive emotions that naturally flow from this practice.

I know how crippling anxiety can feel when we are uninformed and unequipped. But this is also why things quickly turn around when people learn the practical knowledge and skills they can easily remember and apply in their lives. You now have the playbook for making your anxiety a thing of the past. First, set a clear intention to transcend anxiety. Then, start using the skills you've learned, reap the benefits, and let the momentum take care of the rest. You've got this.

Final Thoughts

You now have all you need to start freeing yourself from anxiety. When you are no longer bombarded with feelings and thoughts of self-criticism and self-hatred, you will stop feeling the urgency to fix yourself. As some of my clients did, you might ask, "What if I get complacent and settle? I want to keep becoming a better person." That's a good question. My answer is that everything is an experiment. You can test the hypothesis (i.e., if I'm more at peace and happy with myself, I'll stop improving) by following the steps outlined in this book and transcending anxiety. If you find that you are getting complacent and don't like the new, probably happier and healthier you, then you can easily go back to the way you were. Just start avoiding, worrying, what-if-ing, and catastrophizing, and you'll get your anxiety back in no time!

In all seriousness, I'm willing to bet that freeing yourself from anxiety will make you want to grow and work on yourself more than ever because you'll start to enjoy life more and be eager to explore the uncharted territories now made available to you. Can you imagine what it would be like when you are free to be exactly who you are and feel good about it? I dare say that transcending anxiety is an exciting, worthwhile journey. Keep going. Freedom awaits you.

Appendix: For Further Reading

On Neuroscience of Anxiety

1. Rewire Your Anxious Brain: How to Use the Neuroscience of Fear to End Anxiety, Panic, and Worry, *by Catherine M. Pittman, PhD and Elizabeth M. Karle, MLIS*

2. Keeping the Brain in Mind: Practical Neuroscience for Coaches, Therapists, and Hypnosis Practitioners, *by Shawn Carson and Melissa Tiers*

3. Buddha's Brain: The Practical Neuroscience of Happiness, Love, and Wisdom, *by Rick Hanson*

On Acceptance and Self-Compassion

1. Self-Compassion: The Proven Power of Being Kind to Yourself, *by Kristin Neff, PhD*

2. Radical Compassion: Learning to Love Yourself and Your World with the Practice of RAIN, *by Tara Brach*

On Mindfulness

1. Wherever You Go, There You Are: Mindfulness Meditation in Everyday Life, *by Jon Kabat-Zinn*

2. Buddha's Brain: The Practical Neuroscience of Happiness, Love, and Wisdom, *by Rick Hanson*

On Emotional Freedom Technique

1. The Tapping Solution: A Revolutionary System for Stress-Free Living, *by Nick Ortner*

On Self-Hypnosis and Visualization

1. The Self-Hypnosis Solution: Step-by-Step Methods and Scripts to Create Profound Change and Lifelong Results, *by Richard Nongard*

2. Creative Visualization, *by Shakti Gawain*

References

Bartlett, Andrew A., Rumani Singh, and Richard G. Hunter. "Anxiety and Epigenetics." *Advances in Experimental Medicine and Biology* 978: 145–66 (2017). https://doi.org/10.1007/978-3-319-53889-1_8.

Davis, Michael, David L Walker, Leigh Miles, and Christian Grillon. "Phasic vs Sustained Fear in Rats and Humans: Role of the Extended Amygdala in Fear vs Anxiety." *Neuropsychopharmacology* 35 (1): 105–35 (2009). https://doi.org/10.1038/npp.2009.109.

Farias, Miguel, and Catherine Wikholm. "Has the Science of Mindfulness Lost Its Mind?" *BJPsych Bulletin* 40 (6): 329–32 (December 2016). https://doi.org/10.1192/pb.bp.116.053686.

Farias, M., E. Maraldi, K. C. Wallenkampf, and G. Lucchetti. "Adverse Events in Meditation Practices and Meditation-Based Therapies: A Systematic Review." *Acta Psychiatrica Scandinavica* 142 (5): 374-393 (August 2020). https://doi.org/10.1111/acps.13225.

Gottschalk, Michael G., and Katharina Domschke. "Genetics of Generalized Anxiety Disorder and Related Traits." *Generalized Anxiety Disorders* 19 (2): 159–68 (2017). https://doi.org/10.31887/dcns.2017.19.2/kdomschke.

Hebb, Donald O. *The Organization of Behavior: A Neuropsychological Theory.* New York: Wiley, 1949.

Jia Jiang, *Rejection Proof: How I Beat Fear and Became Invincible Through 100 Days of Rejection* (New York: Harmony, 2015).

Krill, Patrick R., Ryan Johnson, and Linda Albert. "The Prevalence of Substance Use and Other Mental Health Concerns among American Attorneys." *Journal of Addiction Medicine* 10 (1): 46–52 (2016). https://doi.org/10.1097/adm.0000000000000182.

LeDoux, Joseph. 2007. "The Amygdala." Current Biology 17 (20): R868–74. https://doi.org/10.1016/j.cub.2007.08.005.

Linsambarth, Sergio, Rodrigo Moraga-Amaro, Daisy Quintana-Donoso, Sebastian Rojas, and Jimmy Stehberg. "The Amygdala and Anxiety," in *The Amygdala - Where Emotions Shape Perception, Learning and Memories*, edited by Barbara Ferry. IntechOpen, 2017. https://app.dimensions.ai/details/publication/pub.1090370587.

Lodge, Barbara Straus. "A Call for Kindness, Connection, and Science." *Journal of Substance Abuse Treatment* 141 (October 2022): 108839. https://doi.org/10.1016/j.jsat.2022.108839.

National Institute of Mental Health. "Any Anxiety Disorder," *National Institute of Mental Health*, accessed January 20, 2023, https://www.nimh.nih.gov/health/statistics/any-anxiety-disorder.

O'Hare, David. *Heart Coherence 365: A Guide to Long Lasting Heart Coherence* (France: Thierry Souccar Editions, 2014).

Pittman, Catherine M, and Elizabeth M Karle. *Rewire Your Anxious Brain: How to Use the Neuroscience of Fear to End Anxiety, Panic, & Worry*. Oakland: New Harbinger Publications, 2015.

Pew Research Center. *Most U.S. Teens See Anxiety and Depression as a Major Problem Among Their Peers*. February 2019.

Reddan, Marianne Cumella, Tor Dessart Wager, and Daniela Schiller. "Attenuating Neural Threat Expression with Imagination." *Neuron* 100 (4): 994-1005.e4 (2018). https://doi.org/10.1016/j.neuron.2018.10.047.

Schiele, M. A., and K. Domschke. "Epigenetics at the Crossroads between Genes, Environment and Resilience in Anxiety Disorders." *Genes, Brain and Behavior* 17 (3): e12423 (2017). https://doi.org/10.1111/gbb.12423.

Schlosser M, Sparby T, Vörös S, Jones R, Marchant NL. "Unpleasant meditation-related experiences in regular meditators: Prevalence, predictors, and conceptual considerations." *PLOS ONE* 14(5): e0216643 (2019). https://doi.org/10.1371/journal.pone.0216643

Tseng, Julie, and Jordan Poppenk. "Brain Meta-State Transitions Demarcate Thoughts across Task Contexts Exposing the Mental Noise of Trait Neuroticism." *Nature Communications* 11 (1): 3480 (2020). https://doi.org/10.1038/s41467-020-17255-9.

About the Author

Jacqueline Y. Chu took a deep dive into healing and personal transformation after suffering from anxiety and depression during her legal career. As a criminal lawyer, she witnessed how unaddressed trauma and mental health issues perpetuate a cycle of pain and suffering for those who hurt others and themselves. Through this experience, she found her calling to help people free themselves from the prison of their own minds, and her journey took her to study counselling psychology, meditation, hypnosis, consciousness, and spirituality. Jackie guides people to transform their mental health challenges into stepping stones for healing and growth to reclaim their lives. You can visit her online at jychu.com.

Speaking & Workshops

Jacqueline Y. Chu is available for speaking engagements such as keynotes, interviews, and workshops.

To discuss, contact Jackie through her website jychu.com or by email at jacqueline.chu@jychu.com.

Manufactured by Amazon.ca
Bolton, ON